HAPPINESS + PASSION + PURPOSE

HAPPINESS + PASSION + PURPOSE

Michelle Raz M.Ed., BCC, CSS

Cover Design by Darja Filipovic.

Interior layout and design by www.writingnights.org.
Book preparation by Chad Robertson.
For information about permission to reproduce selections from this book, email michelle@razcoaching.com.

Or write:

    Att: Michelle Raz
    PO Box 771726
    Steamboat Springs, CO 80477

ISBN: 9781795530170

Printed on acid free paper in the United States of America.

24   23   22   21   20   19   8   7   6   5   4   3   2   1

I am eternally grateful for all of my past, current and future clients who have had the courage to embark on a self-improvement journey with me. This book is for YOU.

In Life, You Get What You Think

I think I can't so I don't
I think I'll lose so I quit
I think I'll fail so I give up
I think I'm unlucky so I miss out
~ ~ ~ Think your way to failure

OR

I think I can so I DO
I think I'll win so I TRY
I think I'll succeed so I Persist
I think I'm lucky so I Prevail
~ ~ ~ Think your way to success

– Michelle Raz

CONTENTS

FOREWORD

If we are really lucky, we may run into an "Interpreter" in this lifetime. I mean to describe a special person. A person who is able to take confusing details and interpret them to someone facing the topic with a blank slate. I believe that Michelle Raz is such an Interpreter, and she has given us all the gift of her abilities in this new book.

When I first met Michelle, she was a student in my ADHD Class for Coaches. These coaches were seeking to learn the tools necessary to work on career and life planning issues with their clients. Michelle quickly stood out from the crowd as someone who was thirsty for knowledge, and who went the extra mile because what she was doing was that important to her.

It was clear that career coaching was her true passion. She excelled. She was able to produce life-changing results for clients who had previously struggled to keep jobs or to complete school programs. I knew I had to continue to mentor her, and encourage her to share her methods with the world.

I myself was blessed to be mentored by both Donald E. Super, "the Father of Career Development," and Richard Bolles, author of *What Color Is Your Parachute?* Both men pioneered the idea of self-knowledge as the gateway to the career you were made for, and Richard was kind enough to write the foreword for my own career development book twelve years ago.

Though neither of these great men is still with us today, I have strived to pass on their teachings to Michelle to enable her to bring their wisdom to the next generation. In this book, she has built upon their teachings and mine—and updated them to include new tools, resources, and career paths made possible by recent technological advances.

Michelle also created her own tools—like this book and the webinars she teaches—to help career-seekers learn to identify the attributes of a career they will love, and to use the latest resources to hunt down and acquire careers that fit this bill.

I have been thrilled to have the privilege of teaching Michelle—as my mentors taught me—and the privilege of encouraging her to share this book with you.

Wilma Fellman M.Ed., LPC

ACKNOWLEDGEMENTS

I owe the motivation for writing this book to Wilma Fellman. As a mentor, she inspired me to reach far beyond my own expectations as a writer and contributor to the field of career coaching.

I first encountered Wilma in a course she taught for coaches interested in the career-planning field. It felt like a natural fit for me as I'd been working with many college students who struggled with the executive skills required to succeed in college.

I had developed long-term relationships with many clients who wanted to pursue careers beyond college and were having a hard time making their education work for them. Wilma's course provided me with a systematic approach for coaching a range of people who did not know what they wanted to do with their own careers due to job displacement or job burnout. I began working through the foundational work Wilma developed and adjusting them with/for individual clients.

I expanded the range of services I offered, and created a webinar. Wilma was instrumental as my own coach. She has been a positive influence propelling me to deliver my best work.

Wilma has an innate ability to see your own purpose and path and help you fuel your passion towards meeting that goal. She picked up on subtle cues where I needed encouragement or clarification, and gave it in such a way that I felt it was my own. By the end of the journey, we began discussions on collaborating on this book.

Her influence is felt deeply in every chapter of this book. I am deeply grateful for all her firm and gentle guidance.

Michelle

INTRODUCTION

Are you satisfied with your current career? Do you feel overwhelmed, lost, or stuck seeking out the RIGHT career for you?

Whether you're struggling in the early stages of a career, or struggling to find satisfaction in the one you have, this book is for you!

Navigating the career world can be tough. There are always challenges or obstacles that make it harder for you to connect the dots and get to a career you love. As a career and life coach specializing in working with people who face various challenges (AND who DOESN'T face challenges?) I help people discover a career path that is unique and authentic to their strengths and that leads to a happier, more fulfilled life.

Like you, I spend a lot of time talking with my friends. I spend lots of time speaking with my clients as well. Both groups report numerous life challenges. Many of them felt like failures after unsuccessful career choices or academic programs—only to discover later that the career they excelled in played to their strengths. The discovery amounted to a life changing epiphany for each one of them.

I help people like you discover a career path that is unique and authentic to their strengths. When I coach clients, I assist them to create a strategy for making their goals happen. This is different from a plan. A plan is what a goal has defined. I plan to go to college and become a psychologist. The strategy will be the steps you are going to take along the way to get you there. Another example: the goal of the person reading this book is to find the career they're most passionate about. The strategy is to read each chapter, complete the exercises, and make the connections that point to the ideal career and life path for you.

Stress and life challenges can rob us of our memories of success and encourage us to focus solely on our weaknesses. That focus makes us afraid to pursue a new career. We often overlook our own strengths, so we are often blind to how our own life story already contains seeds of a career we will love.

This book is a step-by-step guide. The exercises and tools herein will answer powerful questions. You will complete meaningful activities that will turn your fear and frustrations into inspiration. You'll learn how to make meaningful connections in your life, and create *your* truly passionate career.

My soulful approach helps you see all the possibilities in yourself through an in-depth exploration of all the essential pieces that make up your unique purpose. I know from experience that each person has a gift to give back to the world, and that we are most fulfilled when we are doing what we are meant to do.

There are opportunities everywhere—so many that we often miss the ones that are right for us, or see them as unrealistic. By stepping back and seeing how your life-experiences, skills, aptitudes, accomplishments, and challenges interact to produce the whole picture of you, you will be able to target and actively hunt down those opportunities that fit you best.

I often tell clients that I gain as much from coaching as they gain from me. Helping people find solutions to their career development challenges is my personal purpose—the mission that fulfills me.

Read this book to learn more about your own!

We will unpack the box of expectations you grew up with, and examine insightful connections between values, personality, strengths, dreams, and goals. You will soon begin to see a pattern formed by all the pieces of yourself. That pattern points to the career that best fits you.

From soul-searching self-discovery, to tips and tricks for networking and interviewing, the exercises and real life stories told here will empower you to create the life and career you will love.

First we'll find ourselves, then we'll find Happiness + Passion + Purpose in the ideal career for you!

Michelle

PART I

WHAT CAREER WOULD SUIT ME BEST?

CHAPTER 1
DESIGNING YOUR
PERSONAL PURPOSE

The privilege of a lifetime is
to become who you truly are.
– Carl Jung

The first step in our journey to a career you love is to define your own personal purpose. This will be a guide. A guide you create by defining what you want from your life. If that sounds heavy, don't worry! We're going to take it step by step.

WHY DEFINE MY PURPOSE?

I hope you are reading this book because you want to find a career that makes you happy. Defining your life purpose allows you to choose your destination, and begin drawing the map you'll need to get there—a better option than taking the first obvious career that falls into your lap.

When you act without purpose, you risk being reactive—you're responding to events around you and not being a *proactive* decision-maker.

You can create a proactive life by learning about yourself and applying your self-knowledge to your career decisions. Consciously determine your likes, dislikes, plans, and goals.

We are all a combination of our genetic traits, our innate skills and talents, and our personal history and experiences. These factors work together to determine which career is easiest for us to find ourselves in, and which is the best fit for us. These two are often not the same.

Personal history includes our expectations—what we are familiar with, or what seems realistic or unrealistic to us. For example, if you grew up around doctors a career path that ends with you becoming a doctor yourself may seem realistic. However, if when you were growing up you didn't have doctors as family members or family friends, becoming a doctor might seem out of reach. This expectation has nothing to do with your choices, or your innate potential.

While these learned attitudes can be useful, they can stop us from pursuing well-suited careers. It is so incredibly important to consciously analyze both what you enjoy, and what you want out of a career. Only then should you investigate which careers will allow you to best fulfill your purpose.

When you live with purpose, you become passionate about living. You are in touch with your drives, and passions; the purpose you've chosen keeps you focused and motivated. Creating this personal purpose is the first step in making the most of your life.

In the chapters that follow, you will learn about some of my clients: Josh, Brad, Megan, Aja, Rose and Tara. All of them initially struggled with feelings of inadequacy, or the fear that the right job for them didn't exist. That is until they learned more about their own life purpose, and from there, what career options were available for them. Today, all of them are thriving in jobs they had once considered impossible.

Josh was a college student who was failing out of his degree program in neuroscience when I met him. His grades fell so low college administrators placed him on academic probation. His school advised him to attend a community college to boost his grades. Sadly, he did not do any better there.

When I met him, Josh felt like he did not belong in college at all and had started to believe he was a failure. He'd become depressed about his future, and his family was desperate to help him.

My job was: "Strategies to help Josh succeed in college." Because he'd been diagnosed with ADHD, his family assumed it was simply a matter of developing compensatory academic skills. However, I had a hunch something else was at the core of his struggles. We did work on his organizational, and time management, skills, but we also investigated whether neuroscience was the right field for him.

Josh's ACT science scores were very high. At that time, neuroscience was a new and very popular undergraduate degree field. Career counselors were encouraging students to pursue it as a doorway to medical school. But a high ACT score in science can indicate a lot of things. Science is an incredibly diverse career and field of study. Many different types of curiosity can lead to high science scores. Moreover some of my clients end up thriving in careers that did not reflect their ACT scores. Standardized test scores do not always accurately tell you what your skills and strengths are.

Instead of assuming that Josh's struggle came from a simple lack of academic skill, I took him through some exercises. I wanted to identify his strengths and interests. Only a few exercises in, it became evident that Josh had intense passion and strength—just not in neuroscience!

It turned out Josh had always dreamed of working in the investigative field. He talked excitedly about how he had wanted to be a detective like Sherlock Holmes growing up. As he got older, he assumed that this was unrealistic, because he didn't know any people in the real world who were investigators, or who solved mysteries.

Josh's personal experience did not tell him the whole story—those careers do exist, and there was no reason he couldn't have one.

Rediscovering this passion, he went home and spent hours researching the career fields where such investigative skills were essential. In the end, he decided to switch majors and study Global Security—a field that involves gathering intelligence, and putting diverse chunks of information together like pieces of a puzzle. It meant keeping people safe, just like

Josh's favorite detectives.

Initially Josh saw his career transition challenges as insurmountable. His GPA was low, which made other schools skeptical that he would succeed if they accepted him. More importantly, Josh had internalized the idea that he was just "bad at school." That made him hesitant to apply for enrollment.

With the help of strategic planning to raise his GPA, and consults with the right academic officers, he applied and was admitted to a Global Security studies program.

For Josh, the difference between studying something he loved and something he had been told to study was incredible.

Last I checked in with Josh, he was attending graduate school with a near perfect GPA!

I have no doubt Josh will do incredibly well in a career he loves. Imagine though, how things may have been had he not found what he was passionate about.

PASSION AND PURPOSE TASK 1.1: INVESTIGATE YOUR INNER NARRATIVE

In this section, you'll find questions that help you identify your passions. Spend some time with these questions. Get into the headspace of paying attention to your own joys and strengths, with a sharp eye out for *why* these things make you happy.

To get the most from these questions, you'll need to answer them honestly—even if what you truly feel seems "silly" or "unrealistic." We learned from Josh's journey that countless skills and passions make the world go round, and that seemingly unrealistic goals may actually be perfect for *us*. So give yourself honesty. You need honesty to get matched with the best career for you!

- What motivates me in life?
- What have I wanted, but never gotten, in life?
- What energizes me? How?
- What brings me the most joy? Why?
- What are my biggest interests?
- What do I REALLY, REALLY want in life?
- Who do I enjoy being around? Why?
- How can I turn these loves and desires into a statement of purpose for the next several years of my life?

Is there a passion, skill, or craft you want to devote your life to perfecting? Is there an area of study you want to devote your life to advancing? Is building wealth your top priority? Or is there a challenge you'd like to devote your life to helping others overcome?

There are countless possible answers, but some could look like this:

- My purpose in life is to help end world hunger.
- My purpose in life is to help people look and feel their best.
- My purpose in life is to empower others through education.
- My purpose in life is to care for the sick.
- My purpose in life is to become an artist whose work moves people.
- My purpose in life is to change laws and policies to create a better world.
- My purpose in life is to build as much wealth as possible for my family and future generations.

Consider that different skills may fulfill the same purpose. Which way of contributing might suit you best? Are you a people person, for instance, or do you prefer to work alone? Do you like to do hands-on work, or do you prefer to study and work out theories?

For example:

- A person could help end world hunger by being a scientist, a politician, or a founder or employee of an organization devoted to hunger relief.
- A person could help others to look and feel their best as a fitness trainer, a cosmetologist, a nutritionist, or a fashion designer.
- A person could empower others through education as a schoolteacher, a founder or staff member of an adult or extracurricular education program, or a producer of educational media.

If you find yourself having difficulty defining your purpose, think about reframing the questions with these pointers:

- If you knew you only had had 6 months to live, what would you want to do with that time?
- If you were not responsible for anyone but yourself, what would you do with your time?
- When you die, what do you want your obituary to say about you?

PASSION AND PURPOSE TASK 1.2: GOALS

Now that you've gotten the creative juices flowing, consider breaking down your thoughts into goals—career or otherwise—that you would like to focus on achieving in the next few years. List at least five.

1.
2.
3.
4.
5.

Once you have made this list, consider some new questions:

- Why are you doing what you are doing?
- What do you want to get out of this?
- What differences will this goal make in you, or in your life?

PASSION AND PURPOSE TASK 1.3: PERSONAL MANIFESTO

Write yourself a personal statement that defines your personal purpose. It doesn't have to be fancy or long; a paragraph's worth will do. But it should be something that makes you excited about the path you describe. This is a real path forward in your life and you are excited about it!

Consider printing it out and placing it somewhere you can see every day—someplace easily accessible. Career development comes with many challenges and discomforts. When you feel like stopping, go back to your personal manifesto. Allow it to invigorate you. Remind yourself why you're doing all this.

Congratulations! You've just taken your first step toward career development.

KEY TAKEAWAY

Defining your personal purpose helps you choose your goals and reach them.

Download your FREE PDF workbook that includes all of these tasks at
http://www.razcoaching.com/happiness-tasks

CHAPTER 2
THE IMPORTANCE OF HONESTY

"Our lives improve only when we take chances—and the first
and most difficult risk we can take
is to be honest with ourselves."
– Walter Anderson

Creating your life purpose takes into account your true authentic self. In order to understand who you truly are, you must take an honest look at all the pieces of your life that make you who are today. What are your triggers? What makes you happy, sad, angry? What is it about your past that makes you who you are today? Even the bad has shaped you in some way that makes you stand out as a unique person today—giving you strengths.

As a child, I spent a lot of time at our family beach house on the shores of the Oregon coast. It was a rustic log cabin sitting on the cliff of a sandy bank. A wooden staircase plummeted down the sandy bank to the ocean. If you walked out about 100 yards, there was a large rock I discovered when I was seven. If you timed it just right, you could climb the rock and sit there until the tide came back in. I would sit there and receive the beauty and calmness of the universe. It was where

I dreamt about my life purpose and how I was going to act and live as an adult.

It has taken me many years to see the thread of my life journey as dating back to that rock. I can see the horizon, stormy clouds, fierce foamy waves at my feet, and the tranquility of sea out in the distance. I can sense the calm I felt at seven years old. This is my go to when I ask myself these questions about my actions, my motivations, and about how my life would be different without them. This place is my "rock"— my centeredness that talks to me even now in a loving and guiding way to help me find my next move in life. If you find yourself in a position where you cannot seem to answer the questions. I urge you to go back in your memory to a place that made *you* feel safe or comfortable. A place that you could be you without judgment or fear to say aloud your fears and dreams, and ask for guidance. This connection from the past helps me relate to situations that arise today. If I can go back to that inner child, that feeling of contentment, to knowing that the future was what I wanted and chose to create, then I can honestly answer the questions that I have posed. The answers are coming from my true authentic self.

The word that comes to mind for me is tenacity. If you have tenacity then you have the strength to overcome any challenges you may face in your life today. Be persistent with yourself and ask the questions. The past is a part of a building block that lays the foundation to overcoming the hurdles you face. Use your personal stories to weave the life you want by drawing from the positive attributes of your life experiences.

Who you are today is a result of all the experiences contained in your personal history.

Passion and Purpose Task: Reflection Focus

- Think of personal space you had growing up. Why was it special to you?
- Where was it? Can you visualize it?
- What did it make you feel when you visited it?
- What things did you ponder there?
- How was it important to you?
- How did it help you?
- How can this connection help you now?

Key Takeaway
Use awareness of your history to create your desired future.

Download your FREE PDF workbook that includes all of these tasks at
http://www.razcoaching.com/happiness-tasks

CHAPTER 3
SELF-KNOWLEDGE AND AWARENESS

The unexamined life is not worth living.
– Socrates

Now that you've defined your life purpose, you can begin to hone some career development components. Self-knowledge is the foundation of career development.

CREATING SELF AWARENESS

Learning about yourself is important to this process.

We are all a combination of unique interests, accomplishments, aptitudes, values, personality attributes, drive, work habits, and career dreams. The following exercises allow you to pull together all the aspects of yourself so as to open up a world of opportunities.

My clients often get incredibly excited as we explore their likes, dislikes, and behavioral patterns. Things like whether they like to sit at a desk or prefer to move around, or whether they prefer working with people to working alone. Many tell me nobody asked them these questions before!

Sometimes my clients already have a preferred career. Many already have impressive qualifications; they just aren't happy with their current job. They're looking for a change.

Very often, we are able to find clients different career paths within the same field. That's because most fields have many discrete jobs, each with its own suite of roles and requirements. There are usually as many discrete jobs as there are personality types who might enjoy them.

Someone conducts research in the lab, for instance, and someone else has to turn the findings into practical benefits by telling other people about discoveries resulting from that research. Someone has to give political speeches, and someone else has to quietly strategize finding the right audiences.

Read on to learn about Brad, a client who was miserable in what he thought was his dream job until he learned about other careers that would value his expertise.

PERSONALITY TYPES

Brad was extremely intelligent. He was enthusiastic about computer science, and he excelled at it. After graduating with a master's degree, he became a researcher focused on the latest computing developments.

But once he became a researcher—what he thought was his dream job—he began to come home from work feeling drained. Depression followed. He could not find the motivation to go to work. His numerous absences led to his termination.

Many people, looking at Brad's situation from the outside, were baffled by this turn of events. Brad was highly motivated, passionate, and did very good work. Why in the world would he become depressed, or perform poorly on the job?

As it turned out, Brad had a very social and extroverted personality. He needed to be around people. People energized him. Brad's personality was unsuited to the research job he had, which had him spending his days alone at a computer terminal. It was his personality, not his ability, that was misaligned with his career! As with Josh, this misalignment threatened to make Brad feel incompetent and caused him to question his capabilities. In reality, Brad had the perfect strengths—for a different job.

When Brad and I started working together, we researched personality types and applied what we learned to realign his career. He springboarded from researcher to computer science business consultant.

In this new role, he spent his days meeting new people and helping them find the best computing solutions for their business. His unusually outgoing personality worked together with his computer science expertise to make him a spectacular consultant. Brad thrived in his new job.

Many factors contribute to who you truly are—genetics, socioeconomic factors, life experiences. Your personality is the sum of these influences. Your personality affects the kinds of work environments you feel comfortable in, how you interact with people, the types of tasks you enjoy, and what work style best motivates you. For this reason, understanding your personality is incredibly helpful in revealing the type of career where you will excel.

This chapter takes you through some basic questions and exercises to help you learn more about your personality, as it applies to the career world.

While it may be worthwhile to learn to do things you don't enjoy or struggle with, there is no reason to struggle for career fulfillment like Brad. Brad got trapped by the belief that "researcher" was the *only* role in the computer science field.

It is always worth investigating whether there is a career that works well with *all* the aspects of your personality.

PASSION AND PURPOSE TASK 3.1:
EVALUATE YOUR PERSONALITY

The following are a few scenarios that demonstrate some of the differences in personality types. Put a check mark beside the scenario that applies to you most of the time.

Type A

_____ You prefer to interact with people

_____ You "process" problems by talking about them with others

_____ You find interruptions to be a blessing

_____ You prefer working with a group to working alone

_____ You are thought of as talkative

_____ You think out loud

Type B

_____ You prefer to read and think, rather than talk about how to solve a problem

_____ You are annoyed by interruptions

_____ You prefer working on tasks alone to working with groups

_____ You think first, then speak after you have decided what you are going to say

_____ You are quiet while others lead and organize

_____ You "process" best on your own

Are you more A or B? _____

Type C

_____ You notice details

_____ You need concrete evidence to believe something

_____ You like following a step-by-step process

_____ You seldom make errors

Type D

_____ You might miss details

_____ You don't need concrete evidence, but rather reach conclusions based on "instinct"

_____ You don't like following a step by step process, and might improvise or jump ahead

_____ You often miss things or make errors

Are you more C or D? _____

Type E

_____ You decide things using facts

_____ You can work amid social tension

_____ You might say things that hurt people's feelings

_____ You can tell others what to do

Type F

_____ You decide things using feelings

_____ You need social harmony at work

_____ You try to please others and make them comfortable

_____ You'd rather do something yourself than tell someone else to do it

Are you more E or F? _____

Type G

____ You manage time well

____ You hate schedule changes

____ You prefer to know what will happen next

____ You like the sense of completion that comes from finishing a project

____ You prefer things organized

Type H

____ Your time sometimes seems to vanish without anything getting done

____ You welcome surprise changes and developments

____ You prefer a flexible lifestyle

____ You like keeping a project going

____ You prefer things laid back

Are you more G or H? _____

Download your FREE PDF workbook that includes all of these tasks at
http://www.razcoaching.com/happiness-tasks

Type A is the External Type. You thrive in social situations. External types draw energy from others. Careers that involve a lot of contact with the public, or other team members, might be a good fit for you. Consultants, salespeople, service industry professions, and public relations people are some examples of professions you might be especially good at.

Type B is the Internal Type. You are best in situations that allow you to process information and decide how you want to interact with other people. This doesn't mean you aren't social. It means that you thrive when you have space for your own reflections and thoughts. You may work best when you can do independent work and then bring the information to a team. Consider jobs that allow for this type of balance—researcher, technical professional, writer, editor, or administrator.

Type C is the Detail Type. Your senses are especially fine-tuned. Sensory impressions make lasting imprints on your memory. This makes you especially good at processing immediate and existing situations, while you may be less interested in working with "general principles" and hypotheticals. Detail types may do well as schoolteachers, law enforcement officers, skilled craftspeople, and inspectors.

Type D is the Overview Type. You might feel that you often miss details, and prefer overall-picture and big-idea situations. You might be more interested in discovering the general principles undergirding how things work, rather than slogging through the details. You may do well in research, as a musician, or historian.

Type E is the Head Type. You enjoy situations and duties where you can make decisions based solely on the facts at hand and avoid getting bogged down by emotions. You make decisions from your head and can separate business from personal matters. You are able to make firm leadership decisions, even the uncomfortable ones. Careers where this is helpful include corporate business, human resource departments, management roles, and criminal law.

Type F is the Heart Type. It may be difficult for you to be directly responsible for correcting someone's behavior. Having to transfer a subordinate to another department might likewise be difficult. Seeing someone upset or reprimanded could be very distressing for you. You may do well in a career that involves caregiving, emotional expression, or helping people meet their goals—social worker, counselor, writer, or artist.

Type G is the Structured Type. You are most productive in jobs where you know the expectations and rules of the game. You are reliable and punctual and enjoy deadlines. You prefer consistency, with few surprises, as you work better when you know what to expect. A career fit for you would be a job that requires precision, accountability and structure—medical technician, accountant, or librarian for instance.

Type H is the Unstructured Type. You enjoy the freedom of an unstructured environment that allows you to go with the flow. You hate to keep time and may not even wear a watch. You are most comfortable in an environment where you do not have deadlines and can work on a project continuously until you feel it is done. You would enjoy a job that has many multi-task components so you can keep busy, and can easily flow from one task to another. Jobs that you may gravitate to that fit this type are creative professions such as art teacher, graphic designer, writer, photographer, or independent artist.

We are all a combination of three levels of our personality:

Our disposition. This includes innate traits like introversion or extraversion, whether we prefer academic work or hands-on tasks, whether we like to act based on emotions or on logic, etc. Many of the things that you either just love or hate maybe because of your disposition.

Our personal history. Components include careers we were exposed to growing up; the sorts of schools we had access to as children; as well as the types of careers we were encouraged to pursue when we were young. Our personal history can teach us valuable things but can sometimes also needlessly limit the range of careers that we consider.

Our choices. The choices we make determine many important things about where we end up. For purposes of this book, our choices can include whether we actively seek jobs that work well with our dispositions, or whether we seek career education and resources that will take us beyond the range of possibilities we previously knew.

You can use the self knowledge gained in the previous exercise to make career choices informed by knowledge of their own personality and disposition, and by knowledge of the careers and resources out there to help.

Your Values

Values are the things that are most important to you. They describe what you find most fulfilling, what you absolutely must have, and what you can't do without. Many people find that they are most fulfilled when they focus on what is most important to them, while de-prioritizing less important interests.

Like your personality, your values and how you align them with your work and life will determine your overall sense of well-being, confidence, and satisfaction.

The U.S. Department of Labor's O*NET program identified six core work values. These core values have global representation. Individuals the world over report that they are important to a person's satisfaction.

- **Achievement** — Occupations that satisfy this work value are results-oriented and allow employees to use their strongest abilities, giving them a feeling of accomplishment. Corresponding needs are Ability Utilization and Achievement.

- **Independence** — Occupations that satisfy this work value allow employees to work on their own and make decisions. Corresponding needs are Creativity, Responsibility, and Autonomy.
- **Recognition** — Occupations that satisfy this work value offer advancement, potential for leadership, and are often considered prestigious. Corresponding needs are Advancement, Authority, Recognition, and Social Status.
- **Relationships** — Occupations that satisfy this work value allow employees to provide service to others and work with co-workers in a friendly non-competitive environment. Corresponding needs are Co-workers, Moral Values, and Social Service.
- **Support** — Occupations that satisfy this work value offer supportive management personnel. Corresponding needs are Company Policies, Supervision: Human Relations and Supervision: Technical.
- **Working Conditions** — Occupations that satisfy this work value offer job security and good working conditions. Corresponding needs are Activity, Compensation, Independence, Security, Variety and Working Conditions.

The question to ask yourself is: 'Which of these values are most important to you?'

Some people may value financial security as a way to ensure they have enough money to live comfortably in retirement years. Other people may find that enjoying their daily interactions with coworkers and customers is at the top of their value system. Still, others may value the freedom to make their own decisions and express their own individuality in the workplace.

PASSION AND PURPOSE TASK 3.2:
VALUE CHECKLIST

First, make a list of things you most value in a job. You can also list more values if you like, but remember: the more values you prioritize, the less you'll be able to focus on each one.

1.

2.

3.

4.

5.

Now complete the work values checklist below by marking each listed element as 'Very Important,' 'Moderately Important,' or 'Not Very Important.'

After rating each value, compare the items you identified as 'Very Important' to each other.

Working Alone	_____	Working With Others	_____
Working For Organization	_____	Self-Employment	_____
Well Defined Duties	_____	Room for Creativity	_____
Being One's Own Boss	_____	Working Under Someone	_____
Helping Others	_____	Working with Data	_____
Close Supervision	_____	Little to No Supervision	_____
Low Level of Responsibility	_____	High Level of Responsibility	_____
No Critical Decisions	_____	Making Critical Decisions	_____
30 – 40 hours / week	_____	40+ hours and weekends	_____
Guaranteed Regular Hours	_____	Flexible Hours	_____
Fixing Things	_____	Caring For Others	_____

Close to Home	_____	Traveling	_____
Variety of Daily Tasks	_____	Similar Daily Tasks	_____
Challenges and Risk	_____	Security and Safety	_____
Fast Pace High Pressure	_____	Slow Pace Low Pressure	_____
Visible End Product	_____	Intangible End Product	_____
Short Term Goals	_____	Long Term Goals	_____
Working Indoors	_____	Working Outdoors	_____
Working to Benefit Others	_____	Working to Benefit Self	_____
Formal Dress Code	_____	Casual Dress Code	_____
Opportunities to Relocate	_____	Staying Local	_____
Working for Large Business	_____	Working for Small Business	_____
Working with Machines	_____	Little Work with Machines	_____
Working with Computers	_____	Minimal Computer Use	_____
Early Retirement	_____	Opportunities after 65	_____
Frequent Travel	_____	Little to No Travel	_____
Retirement Savings	_____	Company Benefits	_____
Societal Benefits	_____	Personal Goals	_____
Strong Earning Potential	_____	Excellent Health Benefits	_____
Helping Those with Needs	_____	Working with General Public	_____

Does your 5 most valued in a job exercise match with your "very important" in this checklist? What is your takeaway from this exercise?

PASSION AND PURPOSE TASK 3.3: LEISURE TIME VALUES

What you do in your spare, or leisure, time can tell a lot about your values. Leisure activities include hobbies, casual interests, and relaxation activities. These are activities you do simply because you enjoy them.

If you find that's not the case—that the leisure time activities you list are not activities you enjoy and find relaxing—then you may wish to use the personality inventories in this book to help you choose leisure time activities that satisfy you, too!

To determine how your leisure activities might help you find a career that works for you, answer the questions below:

1. What types of books/magazines do you read, or what movies/TV programs do you watch for pleasure?
2. What activities do you enjoy in your leisure time?
3. What subjects did you, or do you, find most interesting in school?
4. What are your hobbies?
5. What websites do you like to browse?
6. If you could be anywhere you wanted to be right now, where would you be?
7. Have you ever studied a topic in great detail, just for fun because you found it interesting? What was that topic?
8. Have you ever developed a set of skills for fun, just because you wanted to? What were those skills?

Using the answers above, list at least three things that you really enjoy doing, based on your leisure time interests:

1.
2.
3.

Do these activities and interests align with your answers to your personality exercises so far? If so, consider how you may integrate these activities and interests into your work. If not, consider why your answers to questions about what you like to do might be different from what you actually do in your spare time.

Do your hobbies involve skills that might be valuable in certain career fields? Perhaps you have an encyclopedic knowledge of a subject, or you're particularly skilled art or craft? Are you good at solving certain types of problems, or pursuing certain types of goals? Could the things you like to read, watch, or study be valuable to one or more industries?

KEY TAKEAWAY
Understanding the self provides greater likelihood of fulfilling career choices.

CHAPTER 4
DISCOVERING YOUR
CAREER INTERESTS

Life isn't about finding yourself.
Life is about creating yourself.
— George Bernard Shaw

If you already know exactly what you're interested in, congratulations! But many of us may not have thought about this much, or may even have been told that what we are interested in isn't all that important. Indeed, you may have heard people say that it's not possible to love your job, or that it's more important to have a job that makes money than one that you enjoy.

Luckily, neither of those things are true.

While money is one of many values to consider when choosing your ideal career, the truth is that careers allow for a wide range of skills, dispositions, likes, and dislikes. Every industry needs its introverts and extroverts, its academics who like to study, and its people who like hands-on work. Perhaps some of those folks who say it is not possible to love your job are simply in the wrong job for them.

Megan was a classic case of someone who needed to figure out her interests before anything else could line up.

She had ADHD and struggled to pay attention in high school. She often got into trouble for talking or failing to finish assignments. She was very social and did not see herself as academic.

After high school she enrolled in a 4-year college. She knew that was what was expected of her. But she soon found that she did not have passion for academic study, and found it impossible to concentrate. This left her with poor grades and little hope for her academic future.

Feeling defeated and lost, she began to dig into what her true interests and passions were. She realized that when she was a small child, she'd enjoyed dressing her sister, her friends, and dolls. She had even given a friend's American Girl Doll (a very expensive doll!) a haircut. Her friend's mother was distraught over what she'd done to this pricey doll, but even she came around to admitting the haircut was quite good. At eight years old, Megan had a latent talent for the beauty industry. Later in high school, friends would ask her to do their makeup and hair for prom.

With this information in mind, she left the 4-year college and pursued cosmetology school. In a field where her interests were appreciated, she excelled and felt alive in school for the first time. On papers and tests, she now scored the highest marks in her class!

She graduated top of her class, landed a job at the best-rated spa in town, and went on to work at several high-end medical aesthetic spas. She earned top sales, repeat clients, and excellent reviews. Her income proved her excellence as well. The rewards of day-to-day compliments and financial success motivated her to pursue management-level positions. She continues to excel today.

Once she knew what she was passionate about, she was incredibly driven to overcome challenges that stood in her way, and even found new levels of skill to aspire to and achieve!

HOW DO YOUR INTERESTS AFFECT YOUR CAREER CHOICE?

Each of us has our own unique skills and strengths. Our interests help us discover what those are. We're more likely to be interested in things we're good at, and we're more likely to become good at things we find fun. What might be thought of as a 'distraction' or 'hobby' in one career could be an essential skill and professional strength in another.

The challenge for many is finding a career that truly takes advantage of those interests—one where the components of career development corresponding to where your natural strengths are, are allowed to shine.

The psychologist, Carl Jung, wrote about how our inner voices and promptings can lead us in the direction of our greatest strengths. He spoke of individuation—a process by which we discover ourselves as individuals with unique strengths and desires, instead of just extensions of the wishes of our parents or society.

Individuation is a major part of finding a fulfilling career—especially for those of us who may have been told by our parents or by career advisors what *they* think we should do.

EARLY CAREER DREAMS

Think back to your early childhood games, where you chose to act out a character in a career. When we were young and did not think about any limitations of what we 'could be,' we were free to pretend to be whatever we wanted. Let's try to recapture that mindset.

What was that character for you? Where you an astronaut? Doctor? Truck driver? Nurse? If you dreamed of being an astronaut, what was it about this profession that interested you?

Did you dream of the moment you would take off in the spacecraft? Was it the sheer excitement of travel that thrilled you? Was it inquisitiveness about what the world would look like from space? Did you like the idea of being famous or exploring new frontiers?

The answer to these questions can bring insight into your inner interests and motivations, and how best to pursue those in your adult life!

PASSION AND PURPOSE TASK 4.1: DREAM/DAYDREAM CHECKLIST

The goal of this activity is to get in touch with your childhood career dreams. If you have trouble, go to a quiet place and visualize back when you were in preschool or kindergarten and you had a box of dress up clothes in front of you. Think of TV shows or books that you read back then. What were you drawn to?

Check off any of the following if they have ever been one of your early career visions. Feel free to add some that many not appear.

_____	Astronaut	_____	Veterinarian
_____	Nurse	_____	Actor
_____	Teacher	_____	Skater
_____	Firefighter	_____	Professional Athlete
_____	Singer/Songwriter	_____	Inventor
_____	Rock Star	_____	Researcher
_____	Dancer	_____	Writer
_____	Cartoonist	_____	Parent
_____	Lion Tamer	_____	Race car driver
_____	Circus clown	_____	Opera singer
_____	Sales person	_____	Truck driver
_____	Shopkeeper	_____	Musician
_____	Zoo Keeper	_____	Lawyer
_____	Librarian	_____	Scientist
_____	Doctor	_____	_____

What was it about each of these careers that you were drawn to? Try naming three attributes you admire from each of your chosen professions.

What do your chosen career, and your chosen attributes, say about you? Is there any overlap between the characteristics you like in one profession, and characteristics you like in other professions? If so, these attributes might be worth considering—if many of your dream careers have the same attributes, those attributes may be important work values for you!

PASSION AND PURPOSE TASK 4.2:
JOB ACTIVITY TYPES

Check off the types of job activities that would interest you most.

- ☐ Working with my hands
- ☐ Doing research
- ☐ Helping others
- ☐ Making a lot of money
- ☐ Processing data
- ☐ Being a leader
- ☐ Competing with others
- ☐ Writing stories
- ☐ Operating machinery
- ☐ Working regular hours
- ☐ Traveling often
- ☐ Building things
- ☐ Being artistically creative
- ☐ Selling products or service
- ☐ Promoting a product or service
- ☐ Organizing information
- ☐ Making decisions
- ☐ Growing plants, fruits, vegetables
- ☐ Making speeches
- ☐ Being outdoors
- ☐ Changing activities often
- ☐ Speaking a foreign language

- ☐ Fixing things
- ☐ Expressing myself
- ☐ Managing others
- ☐ Doing office work
- ☐ Taking risks
- ☐ Working at my own pace
- ☐ Working with animals
- ☐ Planning events
- ☐ Writing technical material
- ☐ Promoting a service
- ☐ Competing with others
- ☐ Solving problems
- ☐ Teaching others
- ☐ Persuading others
- ☐ Keeping records
- ☐ Learning new things
- ☐ Working with a team
- ☐ Working on a computer writing ads
- ☐ Writing creatively
- ☐ Selling merchandise
- ☐ Raising money for charitable causes
- ☐ Other:

PASSION AND PURPOSE TASK 4.3: SIX INTEREST CLUSTERS FOR CAREERS ACTIVITY

Interest clusters are a way of classifying careers based on the sorts of tasks, skills, and ways of thinking they require.

Interest clusters take task-types into account, things like whether a task is theoretical or hands-on. They also look at personality types, like whether a person is introverted or extroverted, and passion types, such as whether a person is drawn to artistic expression, to helping others, to solving problems, or to discovering new facts.

By putting these parameters together, the interest cluster system can help job-seekers learn a lot about different careers, based on their own personalities, values, and interests.

These tools are based on John L. Holland's career theory and are a foundational part of the U.S. Department of Labor's occupational information system. Career counselors across the United States use Holland's system daily.

The first concept is that all people can be described as a combination of two or more of six personality types: Realistic, Investigative, Artistic, Social, Enterprising, and Conventional.

Once a type-combination is identified, it is referred to as a person's *code*. There are several ways for a person to learn his or her type. One way is to take an assessment instrument. There are also informal ways of learning one's code, such as describing the six types and having the participant select in order of relevance.

The first letter of a person's code tells you the most dominant personality type. The second letter tells you the second most dominant, and so forth. People can list as few as two of their personality types, to prioritize their most important interests and personality traits, or they can list all six in order of importance.

Many career counselors like to use two three-letter codes, which allow people to give strong consideration to the two or three most important types for that person. These two or three letters are a person's "Holland Code."

For example, a "RES" code means the person has a personality and interests that are associated with the Realistic type and, to a lesser extent, has personality and interests that are associated with the Enterprising and Social types.

Holland and others have been doing research in this field for more than forty years. One of the things they studied is the order in which these six types should be organized. And that's where Holland's famous Hexagon comes in.

The letter R can be placed at any point on the hexagon, but once it is placed, the order, in clockwise fashion, must be R, I, A, S, E, C. The system is sometimes called the RIASEC theory for this reason.

Notice the order of these six types. Personality types or jobs that are next door to each other are most alike. For example, people like the 'R' type are most like the 'I' and the 'C' types. On the other hand, types most unlike each other are across the hexagon from each other. The relationships of 'R' to 'S', or 'I' to 'E' for instance.

According to Holland, higher degrees of consistency within personality types can make it easier to make career decisions and maintain career achievement and satisfaction.

As you might surmise from your knowledge of the six different types, there are fewer jobs available that combine opposites (such as 'CA', 'IE', 'RS', and the reverse of these letters).

People with opposite codes might feel torn between doing one kind of work or the other. If jobs that combine these opposites cannot be found, it may be better to assist the individual to choose one of the two areas for work and to attempt to use the other in community, home, or leisure activities.

Most jobs fall into one of six interest clusters. Some jobs combine more than one, and these jobs may be especially good for people who score strongly in both clusters.

List the six interest clusters in order of "most like you" to "least like you".

1. Realistic or practical jobs are "hands on." They usually result in some tangible product at the end of the task.
2. Investigative or probing activities, such as analysis, inquiry, or research, require in-depth focus on one thing for a long period of time.
3. Artistic or creative fields, such as drama, music, writing, art commercial art, graphic arts, involve self-expression
4. Social or assisting fields involve helping others and require you to be interested in working in a service, teaching, or care-giving capacity.
5. Enterprising or business jobs are typically those that require some competitive edge to sell, manage, or persuade others.
6. Conventional or organizing jobs work best for those who are detail oriented and capable of sticking with those details, day to day.

Example
I myself am an SER, using my top three letters from the interest search on www.ONetOnline.org. This translates to career possibilities that include… being a career coach. A good match for my life's chosen work!

PASSION AND PURPOSE TASK 4.4:
OCCUPATIONS OF INTEREST

The complete Dictionary of Occupational Titles (DOT) revised fourth edition, supplied electronically by the US Dept. of Labor at https://www.OccupationalInfo.org is a public service online resource. This is a valuable tool for browsing through various career titles. The site offers complete descriptions and is easily correlated with the career cluster from Task 4.3.

It links with https://www.ONetOnline.org information on jobs and outlooks. These two work nicely together and particularly useful for exploring in-depth information about a particular job. I recommend going further and looking at https://www.MyNextMove.org as well. This will allow for a complete and thorough investigation into jobs, descriptions, educational requirements, skills, salary information, and requisite personal qualifications.

To learn how to use these tools in practice, visit their websites. Explore your interests and read through all the job descriptors. In the space below identify 5 fields that interest you and write them down.

DOT Code Occupational Title
1.
2.
3.
4.
5.

Download your FREE PDF workbook that includes all of these tasks at
http://www.razcoaching.com/happiness-tasks

PASSION AND PURPOSE TASK 4.5: APPLYING SELF KNOWLEDGE

Now that you have a wealth of information about yourself, job types in the world, and what you would like in a job, try visiting some recruitment websites. Pretend that you are looking for your ideal job. Identify five 'the perfect job' candidates.

What excites you about each of your top picks? What makes them look like the perfect job for you? On the other hand, what raises concerns for you, knowing what you now know about your personality, interests, and aptitudes? When you keep a keen eye out for both the pros and cons of any given job, you can make your most educated decisions about which jobs will be best for you. Here is a list of recruiting sites where you can perform your "perfect job" search.

- Monster.com
- Indeed.com
- ZipRecruiter.com
- CareerBuilder.com
- LinkedIn.com
- SnagaJob.com

Job Description	URL	What Interests You	What Concerns You

MORE POSSIBILITIES:

You can further investigate your interests and add to your career map picture by taking any of the standardized tests listed below. These tests are all available online through various resources with varying fees.

If you decide to do these tests online, to get the most from the results, make sure to order a full report. I also recommend seeking versions of these tests that let you discuss their results with a real person—someone who has experience matching people with careers based on their test outcomes.

Alternatively, you may take the results to a career coach who specializes in helping people identify their ideal careers.

Campbell Interest and Skill Survey:

The Campbell Interest and Skill Survey (CISS) measures self-reported vocational interests and skills. Like traditional interest inventories, the CISS interest scales reflect an individual's attraction for specific occupational areas.

Career Assessment Inventory

The Career Assessment Inventory – Enhanced Version assessment compares an individual's occupational interests to those of individuals in 111 specific careers that reflect a broad range of technical and professional positions in today's workforce. Guidance counselors use CISS to help students and adults develop career and study plans. Psychologists and human resource professionals use CISS to advise individuals on career development.

Strong Interest Inventory

The **Strong Interest Inventory** (SII) is a popular career assessment tool. Psychologist Edward Kellog Strong, Jr. developed the test in 1927 to help soldiers transitioning out of the military find jobs.

Hands On Exploration:

Temporary Placement Agencies

Many people have found niche jobs through temporary placement from such job agencies. It can be a low risk experience, allowing you to take on a job temporarily to see if you like it, while getting paid for the experience.

Volunteering

Another option to find out if you like working in a field is to volunteer usually with a non-profit agency, within your interest. This is a great way to test the waters and gain valuable skills—training is frequently provided. Another upside is that your volunteer work could turn into an avenue to long-term employment since you have an edge on any opening that may arise in the organization.

Key Takeaway

Aligning your career with your true interests makes you more likely to succeed in finding a fulfilling job.

CHAPTER 5
MAKING THE MOST OF YOUR EXPERIENCE

Memories are the key, not to the past, but to the future.
– Corrie Ten Boom

Looking at your job history may not be your favorite thing to do. Some people feel like they don't have the experience they had hoped to acquire, or the *right* experience to get them their dream job.

Your résumé may be seen as a stumbling block and disheartening, causing you fear, anxiety and doubt. I like to challenge these feelings and provide connections to possibilities. Many people don't realize they have skills and experience that they can use to portray themselves as the perfect candidate for their career of choice.

Experience in sales, for example, involves skills that may be useful in almost any industry—from retail to politics. If you've ever been self-employed you have business leadership experience, even if you don't have an MBA. If you are chronically ill or have experienced a major injury, you may have valuable experience and understanding of the healthcare field, even if you've never been a healthcare worker or policymaker.

In the chapters to come, we'll practice going beyond official job titles to determine what skills you *really* have, and how to package those for employers.

Looking at your job history is also useful in other ways. Seeing patterns in your job history can help you identify job duties you really enjoy, and the positions it would benefit you to seek out in future.

Tara's story illustrates how skills and experiences can metamorphose into rare combinations of competencies, even if the experiences are not industry-related.

Tara was intimately familiar with the American healthcare system. She had an ADHD diagnosis, and she lived with the ongoing symptoms of a traumatic brain injury. She often experienced mental fatigue and brain fog. That made holding down conventional 9-5 jobs difficult for her.

On top of this, she is a single mother. Tara has two daughters, both of whom struggled with academic and behavioral issues. She needed a job that would allow her to support her daughters, but had flexible hours *and* allowed her to accommodate her cognitive symptoms and her daughters' academic schedules.

At first glance, Tara's work history may not have looked like one that would translate into a high-paying job in a healthcare-related field. To support herself, she had been working as an exotic dancer. To make ends meet, she had been on Medicaid, and on, and off, other public assistance programs, for years.

But Tara was very good at what she did. As a dancer, she was a charismatic performer incorporating public speaking techniques and best practices into her persona. As a long-term patient with chronic health challenges, she'd become very well-acquainted with the healthcare system, as well as the assistance programs and legal protections that were in place for low-income people, and those with chronic illnesses.

She was extremely passionate about improving the plight of other people whose earning potential was limited through no fault of their own. People who were affected by illness, injury, the time and financial pressures of raising children, and a lack of institutional support. She advocated for other people she knew in similar conditions, and had even taken trips to Washington D.C. with social justice organizations to share her story and protest for better treatment of low-income families, and the chronically disabled.

Tara knew she could not support her daughters through their teenage years without a career change. She also knew she had skills and experience that she hadn't had the opportunity to use in the workplace because of her health challenges and limited work history.

She sought assistance from the Department of Vocational Rehabilitation (an excellent resource for those with disabilities or health challenges. We'll discuss later in this book) and was paired with my career coaching service to discuss how she could obtain a stable career that she could work despite her traumatic brain injury symptoms.

I knew as soon as I met Tara that she was a great salesperson and public speaker. It was clear she cared deeply about people, and she spoke about issues she was passionate about with conviction. She was capable of crafting great arguments, giving impressive speeches, and had a remarkable amount of knowledge about the American healthcare system and the support system for low-income and disabled people.

In my work with Tara, we developed strategies to manage her cognitive symptoms and maximize her productivity (some of which you and I will discuss in Chapter 9). We polished her résumé, and set out to search for a job that would allow her to use all of her skills and experiences to their maximum value potential.

Today, Tara is a lobbyist—a voice for the rights of the disabled, a voice for single parents. This is a job that puts her natural gift for communication, her firsthand experience with the healthcare and legal systems, and her passion for helping others, all to good use. Lobbying has flexible hours, enabling Tara to work around her cognitive symptoms, and be available for her daughters except for the small portion of her time she spends traveling.

Many of us sense we have strong skills and unique life experiences that are unappreciated in our current jobs. We'll discuss how to identify these and present them to employers, as well as how to form strategies for working around cognitive or health traits that might pose challenges for us in certain jobs.

PASSION AND PURPOSE TASK 5.1: USE YOUR RÉSUMÉ

For this exercise, use a copy of your résumé. If you don't already have a résumé, or the formatting is not a chronological sampling of your last 3 jobs now's the time to make one. Begin with your most recent employment, and order the document by: Job Title, Date of Employment, Name and Address of Employer.

Remember, employers are interested in *all* your skills, so if there's unpaid activity, a position, an award, or recognition you received within the last five years, feel free to include that under its own heading. Useful headings might include "Volunteer Positions," "Awards," and "Publications."

Look at each of the items on your résumé and try to answer the following questions using what you've learned from previous chapters. You may find it helpful to write down the answers on a separate list or spreadsheet, so that you have all your likes, dislikes, skills, and other important pieces of information together in one group:

- What did you like about the job? What did you dislike?
- What matched well with your personality? What did not?
- What matched with your values and how? What did not and how?
- What made you feel excited to be at work? What made you bored?
- What job duties or skills were you particularly good at? What factors led to your quitting, or being terminated?

ACCOMPLISHMENT AND TRANSFERABLE SKILLS

Now, it's time to think outside the box about your skills and accomplishments. Some important skills may not get official recognition in the form of a job title.

Knowing which of those skills you have, and how to use them in cover letters and interviews, will ensure that you do justice to your strengths.

PASSION AND PURPOSE TASK 5.2: FINDING STRENGTHS

Your unique life includes accomplishments and experiences that can be counted as part of your skillset. These are tangible, marketable, skills and likely very applicable to your career development.

Some skills can be learned, and lead to technical proficiencies or certification. Others may be difficult to train employees in, like problem-solving, emotional intelligence, and multitasking. These abilities don't come with a certificate or degree, but they are very valuable to employers.

In this next exercise, look more broadly at your whole life, not just your work history—even as far back as early childhood if you find that helpful.

You're looking for tangible accomplishments and experiences, work-related or no:

- Is there an event that you participated in that you are grateful for? What was it, and what was your role? Would you like to serve in such a role again if you could?
- Think of a recent conversation that was important. What role did you play? For instance, were you the listener, or arbitrator? Did you do a lot of analyzing or empathizing? What does that say about your interpersonal talents?
- How would others describe you? Try thinking of three positive descriptors (like fun, energetic, dependable, or caring) and three negative ones (perhaps some people have told you that you don't smile enough, that you are stubborn, or that you are *too* nice).

For the negative descriptors, try considering the positive flip-side of those. What some people might describe as "no fun" might be grounds for you to say you are serious and responsible. What some people might consider stubbornness might indicate an unusual level of determination and self-confidence.

Even if you are discouraged because you feel you don't have a certain strength, the opposite trait that you *do* have might be extremely useful for the right career role.

- Can you find contentment with day-to-day life or do you constantly seek to change your circumstances? How do you do either?
- Think of a recent situation where something caught you by surprise. How did you react?
- In uncertain situations how do you respond? Do you make plans or act on instinct? Draw on past experiences or go in with an open mind?
- Think of a situation where you had to deal with conflict. What role did you play? Did it give you an opportunity to stand up for your values?
- How do you influence others in a positive way?
- If you were at your own funeral, how would people describe your strengths?

These questions should help you access concrete experiences that showcase your strengths. This is particularly useful for interviewing, and for writing cover letters. In both scenarios, you get a chance to show off why you are uniquely suited to the position.

There is another reason to use this list.

It is easy to forget our accomplishments. Stress, unsuccessful job outcomes, unhappiness at work, or at home, can add up and take their toll on overall contentment.

Many of us only remember our failures. We tend to forget about our successes. This can rob us of well-deserved confidence. We need confidence to reach for our goals and ambitions, even when we've met many of our past goals.

If you find yourself feeling you have no accomplishments, this can be a good list to look back on. Remember what you *have* done—not just what your job title was. Recall the important skills you exercised and honed.

In addition, just because a job title isn't seen as prestigious doesn't mean it didn't involve skills that could be extremely valuable in the job of your choice.

Now that you've had a chance to reflect on yourself with the powerful questioning exercise earlier, let's put it to work and start to identify your successes so far.

PASSION AND PURPOSE TASK 5.3:
SKILLS AND STRENGTHS

Because many of these questions ask you to think of how someone else sees you, some people find it difficult to answer them. It might help to speak with someone you know on a deep level, and who, hopefully, feels they can be honest with you. This can be a great bonding activity as well as a personal growth and career development activity.

1. What subjects in school were easiest for you? What skills did you possess or learn that enabled you to succeed in these subjects?
2. What hobbies or interests did you excel at? Was there an art, craft, or other skill of any type that you did well at? Was there a topic or skill that you learned a lot about just because you were interested?
3. What strengths do you think your family/friends have seen in you?
4. What strengths do you think your teachers have seen in you?
5. What strengths do you think your employers have seen in you?

Take a moment also to consider a few *weaknesses* other people have seen in you. Remember, every trait involves both a strength and a weakness. If you had a hobby or interest that could be considered some sort of weakness, what kind of strength might be the flip-side of that? If you struggled with reading, did you also notice that you were unusually good at hands-on tasks, or working with visual or auditory materials? If you struggled in art class, could that mean you are rigorous and analytical, which made it hard for you to work with a blank canvas? If you were told you talked too much in class, was that because you were busy making friends?

Here again, consider what strengths might be hidden in *negative* feedback you've received.

6. What adjectives best describe strengths in your personality (i.e. ambitious, friendly, perceptive, etc.)?
7. What are at least five accomplishments you achieved in school, work, hobbies, personal life, or in community/volunteer activities? These can be any accomplishments, no matter what size or how long ago.

Now, what skills were required to accomplish these achievements? Try to think outside the box.

If you helped someone in your personal life, what skills did that require? Did it require being empathetic, problem-solving, or being calm in the face of a crisis? How might those skills apply in the workplace?

If you won a video game tournament, did that game require being resourceful, thinking strategically, or dedicating a lot of time to learning the game's rules or environment? How might those skills be applied in the workplace?

8. What about your job performance sets you apart from most people? Was there anything you noticed your colleagues struggle with that you would assist them with, or that you found easy?

Look over your responses to items 1-8 and list 3-5 of your greatest skills or strengths.

1. _____
2. _____
3. _____

TRANSFERABLE SKILLS

Richard Bolles' author of *What Color is your Parachute?* revealed three groups of skills that employers look for in potential hires: Mental, Interpersonal and Physical skills.

Notice none of these skills are about any one job. We call them 'transferable skills' because they can be transferred to any job.

PASSION AND PURPOSE TASK 5.4: IDENTIFYING TRANSFERABLE SKILLS

In the following exercise, you will identify some of your transferable skills. Circle any skill you feel confident about.

Spend only 3 seconds on each item, so that you work instinctively. Your first reaction is usually correct. If you feel unsure that a skill is strong, pass on it. That way you are only identifying the ones you are certain about.

Mental Skills: I am a person who can _____

Research Information	Interview Others	Observe
Study	Read	Sort
Copy	File	Plan
Organize	Prioritize	Think Strategically
Gather Information	Present Information	Synthesize Information
Transcribe / Take Notes	Write	Keep Records
Manage Money	Calculate	Abstract Ideas Come Up With New Ideas
Memorize	Conceptualize	

Interpersonal Skills: I am a person who can _____

Help Others	Take Instructions From Others	Make Good References For Others	Influence Others	Teach Others
Communicate in Writing	Communicate Orally	Entertain Others	Supervise Others	Serve Others
Train Others	Advise Others	Confront Others	Counsel Others	Motivate Others
Resolve Conflicts	Teach a Group	Perform to a Group	Diagnose and Help	Organize a Group
Entertain a Group	Feed a Group	Persuade a Group	Event Plan for a Group	Negotiate
Inspire	Guide	Access People's Strengths	Access People's Weaknesses	Represent Others
Interpret other's ideas	Guide discussions	Make Presentations	Manage or run a Business	Manage or run an event

Physical Skills: I am a person who can _____

Load / Move	Stack / Carry Objects	Build
Calibrate Machinery	Set up Machinery	Operate Machinery
Assemble Equipment	Disassemble Equipment	Monitor Operations
Sew, Weave, Craft	Cut, Carve, Chisel	Paint, Refinish, Restore
Fashion, Model, Sculpt	Wash, Clean, Prepare	Do Precise Work
Work with Animals	Take Care Of People	Do Fine Detail Work
Expedite	Cook	Manufacture
Repair	Maintain	Construct
Operate Vehicles	Garden / Farm	Computer Skills

Tally your skills. Once you're done, I recommend keeping this list near your résumé. You'll need it as reference whenever you're updating or polishing your C.V. You can use it to describe job functions as well as relevant skills. And, as before, if you're ever feeling you are in a rut, you can refer to this list for inspiration.

Good recordkeeping makes applying for jobs, motivating ourselves, and selling ourselves much easier. Having your strengths and skills already listed, written, and accessible saves time and preserves your forward momentum.

It's a good idea to return to these exercises ever so often. We are always growing our strengths through experience.

Aptitude

Aptitude is your natural ability or inclination in certain areas. These can be physical and/or mental. In the previous exercise you learned your skills which may be learned or natural talents. An aptitude assessment can be a way to discover new areas of potential interests and probability of job success.

Your aptitude for a certain area can be enhanced with exposure and training. Some people may also have a genetic predisposition to certain skills.

Take singing, for instance. Some people are born with a naturally beautiful voice and have a distinct ear for music. Then there are people who enjoy singing and have an ear for music but lack the natural ability to sing on pitch. Sometimes these people take music lessons and enhance their ability to sing with dedicated practice.

PASSION AND PURPOSE TASK 5.5: THE DAT TEST

The most common test used to help people identify strengths and weakness in categories is the Differential Aptitude Test (DAT). It can help you understand why you do well or struggle in certain areas and help guide you in career and educational paths. Not only can it help to identify your aptitude, it can show how you best use it.

To obtain a more in-depth picture of your personal results, you can go to https://www.pearson.com, take the test for a fee, and receive personalized results. These test results can help you identify careers you might enjoy and excel at.

The DAT for Personnel & Career Assessment Subtests helps measure aptitude for success. It evaluates:

- Verbal Reasoning—Measures general cognitive ability for placing employees in professional, managerial, and other positions of responsibility requiring complex thinking skills.
- Numerical Ability—Tests the understanding of numerical relationships and aptitude for handling numerical concepts. Good prediction of success of applicants in such fields as mathematics, physics, chemistry, engineering, and in occupations such as laboratory assistant, bookkeeper, statistician, shipping clerk, carpenter, tool-making, and other professions related to the physical sciences.
- Abstract Reasoning—A nonverbal measure of the ability to perceive relationships in abstract figure patterns. Useful in selection when the job requires perception of relationships among things rather than among words or numbers, such as mathe-

matics, computer programming, drafting, and automobile re-pair.

- Clerical Speed and Accuracy (Paper Administration Only)—Measures the speed of response in a simple perceptual task. This is important for jobs such as filing and coding, and for jobs involving technical and scientific data.

- Mechanical Reasoning—Closely parallels the Bennett Mechanical Comprehension Test and measures the ability to understand basic mechanical principles of machinery, tools, and motion. It is useful in selection decisions about applicants for jobs such as carpenter, mechanic, maintenance worker, and assembler.

- Space Relations—Measures the ability to visualize a three-dimensional object from a two dimensional pattern, and how this object would look if rotated in space. This ability is important in fields such as drafting, clothing design, architecture, art, die making, decorating, carpentry, and dentistry.

- Spelling (Paper Administration Only)—Measures an applicant's ability to spell common English words, a basic skill necessary for success in a wide range of jobs including business, journalism, proofreading, advertising, or any occupation involving written language.

- Language Usage—Measures the ability to detect errors in grammar, punctuation, and capitalization. When Language Usage and Spelling are both administered, they provide a good estimate of the ability to distinguish correct from incorrect English usage, which is important in business communication.

Your awareness of your aptitude will reinforce your confidence, your strengths, and inclination toward a specific field of interests. Remember that you can develop all these strengths, skills, and even attitudes via training and exposure.

Also remember that these tests don't measure many important abilities—people skills, creativity, and physical skills. These tests give you a useful picture of whether you are skilled in their particular areas, but are not designed to measure all-important skills that can influence business and career success.

If you are more interested in comparing your interests and skills to a specific job, I recommend using the extensive career information website https://www.OnetOnline.org. On this website, each job query you enter into the search field allows you to compare the specific qualities needed to be successful in that field, as well as identifies similar jobs or positions.

KEY TAKEAWAY
Keep Record of your own Strengths, Skills, and Potential.

Download your FREE PDF workbook that includes all of these tasks at
http://www.razcoaching.com/happiness-tasks

CHAPTER 6
WORKPLACE
BEHAVIOR

Quality is not an act, it is a habit.
– Aristotle

Spending time in contemplative self-reflection to learn about your work habits is a good investment in both career and personal development. It gives you insight into what you may need to work on to deliver consistent results—for employers, and yourself—and the sorts of traits and track records an employer may be looking for.

Because habits are hard to change, it may be beneficial to work one-on-one with a coach who can help you increase your marketability. If you don't have access to a career coach, it is possible to make habit-building and habit-changing plans and execute them on your own time.

Forming habits that become so second nature as to be effortless takes time. Studies have found that it takes at least twenty-one days for a new habit to take root; some professionals say it can take as many as ninety days.

If an action is important, one that will help you reach your goals, it is a good idea to plan to do it every day for ninety days. That way you ensure that it becomes easy and automatic for you.

Workplace Habits

What type of employee are you? Do you go the extra mile? Even when you're not asked to do so? Do you show up early to work or are you chronically late? Employers want to know that you will be a positive addition to their company, that you have attributes that compliment your job title.

The following exercise will help you clarify desirable employee characteristics you already have—and those you could benefit from working on.

It may be helpful to have someone close to you who feels they can be honest with you fill this out as well, as they may see things you might not be aware of.

PASSION AND PURPOSE TASK 6.1:
20 QUALITIES VALUED BY EMPLOYERS

Below is a list of twenty qualities that employers look for in the people they hire. For each one, give yourself a score from 1 to 5, with 1 being 'not at all like yourself' and 5 being 'most like yourself.' This will bring attributes you can emphasize during a job interview to your attention, and identify attributes you should probably seek to improve.

You may find it useful to make a list of all the attributes where you give yourself a 4 or 5, and a separate list of all the attributes where you give yourself a 1 or 2. These lists will help you notice patterns in your skills, and avoid job descriptions that require many of your weaknesses. Seek out job descriptions where your strengths are a serious asset. Dividing the attributes into two lists may also help you to notice areas where you can improve—areas that might increase your ability to reach your goals, both in and outside of the workplace.

Remember, be honest. Be authentic—no one has *every* possible good habit. Knowing which of these habits are truly your best strengths will help you use those to your advantage.

You may also wish to pick out one attribute at a time to work on. Don't try to improve *all* of them at once—you'll get overwhelmed and make little progress. But if there is an attribute you'd like to obtain or improve, you can use a habit-building activity.

Good Communication	_____
Positive Attitude	_____
Flexible and Adaptable	_____
Strives For Excellence	_____
Good Work Ethic	_____

Accepts Responsibility _____
Produces High Quality _____
Produces High Quantity _____
Highly Reliable _____
Eager to Learn _____
Ability to Problem Solve _____
Takes Initiative _____
Creative _____
Resourceful _____
Enjoys Reading _____
High Energy / Stamina _____
Accurate _____
Attentive to Details _____
Punctual _____
Good Attendance _____
Works Well With Others _____

Armed with the above information, complete the following statements:

My work area strengths are: _____.
My work area weaknesses are: _____.
The work area I would like to improve: _____.

PASSION AND PURPOSE TASK 6.2: WORKPLACE BEHAVIOR CHECKLIST

The following checklist is formatted so as to help you easily define for others how your workplace habits produce results for the company. Score yourself on a scale of 1 to 5, with 1 being 'weak' and 5 being 'strong.'

If you find yourself only giving yourself fives, you probably need to think a little harder about which of these statements feel natural and easy to you, and which feel uncomfortable or uncertain.

Likewise, if you find yourself giving yourself only ones, you should ask a friend, a teacher, or mentor how *they* would rate you on these traits. They probably see strengths that you are missing.

Knowing what tasks or skills feel uncomfortable will also help you avoid jobs where those skills are a major part of the job description. You'll be able to focus on jobs where your preferred skills are most important.

Thoroughness:

_____ I plan well ahead when beginning projects

_____ I'm able to stick with detail-oriented tasks for long periods of time

_____ I think things through carefully before I speak or act

_____ My work is consistently high in quality

Memory:

_____ I'm able to remember details over long periods of time

_____ I'm capable of learning new material without taking notes

_____ I can recall important information under high stress circumstances

Communication:
_____ I get along well with co-workers
_____ I get along well with superiors
_____ I get along well with subordinates
_____ I can communicate well in conversations
_____ I can communicate well in writing
_____ I can give honest feedback to colleagues

Organization:
_____ I'm able to coordinate paperwork or digital files
_____ I'm careful not to make mistakes
_____ I take paperwork, forms, and files in stride and am not easily
overwhelmed
_____ I complete assignments in a timely manner
_____ My work is neat and orderly

Cognitive Strengths
_____ I quickly absorb new material and methods
_____ I read material easily
_____ I have strong math skills
_____ I am able to learn whatever I am taught
_____ I love to learn new things

Flexibility
_____ I'm able to work adapt to changes in scheduling or activities
_____ I'm able to work long hours without losing quality
_____ I'm able to work with environmental distractions
_____ I can shift my focus as needed on the job
_____ I welcome change
_____ I like variety

Interpersonal Skills
_____ I am well liked
_____ I enjoy meeting new people
_____ People come to me for guidance
_____ I have an even temperament
_____ I try to make others feel important and heard
_____ I can get along with difficult people
_____ I can make thing "work out" despite difficulties
_____ I am considered a positive person
_____ I can be firm with others

Using the information above fill out the statements below.
My work area strengths are:
My work area weaknesses are:

Finding a balance between work behavior and your style needs can be different. I had a client, Aja, who worked as an accountant. She was quite good at accounting and genuinely enjoyed it, but her particular workplace wasn't a good fit for her interests and personality.

Aja may have loved numbers, but she was also outgoing, creative, and liked deep interpersonal relationships with her colleagues. The company she worked for had her spending her days by herself, working with dry data. To top it all off she faced frequent sexual harassment from her co-workers.

She could get the job done, but it wasn't an environment that would let her flourish. It was a recipe for burnout. So she sought out career coaching.

After reflecting on her personality, abilities, interests, likes, and dislikes, I encouraged Aja to start reaching out to her art community. In this part of her life, her hobby, she'd made many friends among local artists and knew that many of them not only disliked bookkeeping, they could seriously benefit from help with their accounting and budgeting.

Taking on artists as accounting clients allowed her to work flexibly, to be passionate about the people she worked for, and take on projects at her own pace. It also turned her love for art, her outgoing nature, and her deep interpersonal relationships into serious assets to her business instead of traits she had to fight against to function in her workplace.

Working with artists, Aja felt she was with her own kind. She eventually branched out and started developing relationships that allowed her to showcase her own art as well. We'd gotten to the point where she was using her most marketable skill to support her greatest passion. Now, she flourishes as both a freelance accountant and an artist.

If you're in a job that fails to nurture your passion, how can you bring passion into the workplace, or take the workplace to your passion?

KEY TAKEAWAY
Understand your workplace wants and needs.

Download your FREE PDF workbook that includes all of these tasks at
http://www.razcoaching.com/happiness-tasks

CHAPTER 7
OVERCOMING
CHALLENGES

*If you can't fly then run, if you can't run then walk, if you can't
walk then crawl, but whatever you do you have to keep moving
forward.*
– Martin Luther King Jr.

You've no doubt heard the cliché that "struggle builds character." Many clichés are repeated as often as they are because they're true!

The proudest moments in our lives are often the ones where we accomplished something while simultaneously overcoming adversity. There is truly no substitute for experience when it comes to overcoming challenging situations.

Even with this in mind however, we often have a hard time *remembering* what challenges we have overcome, and *how* we overcame them. We might even forget skills we have in these areas, or what worked last time.

It can be useful to make a list of past challenges—including physical, mental, emotional, and financial challenges—and write down how we overcame each of them. Doing this supplies us with a valuable reminder of our own strengths, and a valuable reminder of skills and experience we can draw on in the future.

Challenges come in countless forms, and they are often outside of our control. We don't get to choose what obstacles or setbacks are thrown into our path. We do get to choose how we respond—and we can use the resources and psychological tricks contained here to stay determined, focused, and well informed, about all the tools we have at our disposal.

When you have these resources, your challenge can be an asset or attribute to use. The rug may be pulled out from under us, but we can still strive for a positive outcome from the situation, all the while conducting ourselves with grit, determination, and skillful and strategic use of our resources.

Take Steve, a man who had his entire lifestyle altered during a skiing accident.

Steve was spending a weekend on the slopes. There was nothing unusual that day—normal weather, safe skiing conditions. Still, disaster struck. Steve hit a slushy patch on the course and landed on his head. He describes the moment he realized he could not feel anything below his neck as sheer panic and disbelief.

Despite having worn all necessary protective gear, his neck snapped rendering him quadriplegic. In a hospital and with his family by his side, he spent months in rehabilitation trying to regain any sense of movement in his hands and arms. It seemed certain, at that point, that his days as an athletic outdoorsman were over.

Steve had been an elite ski racer, an accomplished mountain biker, and rafter. He'd spent his entire adult life enjoying the mountains in the Colorado High Country. Unwilling to give up the activities he loved, he faced this life-changing event with the ultimate can-do attitude. His belief system was that he could enjoy his life to the fullest, with the right accommodations.

Having an abundance of creative and entrepreneurially spirited athletic friends was a blessing. These faithful friends created contraptions to allow him to make his way down the river on a raft with a huge smile on his face.

Steve also reached out and made arrangements to ski with an adaptive program. This was on the same mountain that took his livelihood as a fully functional walking man. Steve knew that countless skiers descend these slopes safely every year, and refused to let his limitations end his dreams of enjoying all that the Colorado Mountains have to offer.

Today, you can still find him on his electric chair cruising the downtown streets of his mountain town greeting friends and acquaintances and even meeting new people. He amazes me every time I see him navigating the rough walkways and many hills (not to mention traffic) in his electric chair.

When I ask him why he doesn't have a telecommunications device attached to him for emergencies, he replies that he is not afraid of what might happen to him. He is going to enjoy every moment he can.

At day's end, you can watch him heading up a steep road that is as steep as any street in San Francisco, retreating to his house—made just for him thanks to his own efforts at outreach, and those of his friends and family who support him.

Steve could have succumbed to feelings of powerlessness and stopped reaching for the ability to do what he loves, in the face of such overwhelming challenges. Instead, he embraced what life had to offer him, and continues to pursue his goals to the best of his abilities. Amazing.

Just like Steve's, stories abound of people leading rewarding careers with substantial cognitive and mobility challenges, including paralysis, missing limbs, and 'invisible disabilities' like Tara's lingering TBI symptoms.

In the exercises below, we'll explore some tools to keep our minds on our goals and accomplishments, and combat any discouragement we may experience when we face challenges or setbacks.

Download your FREE PDF workbook that includes all of these tasks at http://www.razcoaching.com/happiness-tasks

PASSION AND PURPOSE TASK 7.1: CONFRONTING NEGATIVITY BIAS

Negativity Bias is a psychological term that describes our biological need to remember potentially threatening or dangerous situations. For early humans, it was extremely important to remember when they got sick after eating that one berry, or how a lion chased them last time they entered that cave.

As a consequence, our brains pay much more attention to negative experiences than positive ones. This is the same reason we often forget our victories and skills if we don't actively remind ourselves of them.

Our contemporary living situation is very different from the environment where we evolved. Our bad experiences are usually things like being rejected by a potential employer, or not doing as well as we'd like on a test. In these situations, unlike the poison berry situation, the best thing we can do is *repeat* the experience—apply to more jobs or take the test again.

Our brains might tell us otherwise. They might say, "why bother," or even develop a fear of job applications or interviews. But our brains are not the boss of us. As Steve's story shows, it's the other way around. Using tools like those listed here, we can actively manage our thoughts and emotions to produce the outcomes we want.

We can combat our brain's tendency to either give up quickly, or avoid situations that may offer us great rewards. We do this by ensuring that we remember our strengths, accomplishments, goals, and strategy.

To balance out your brain's negativity bias, use a journal to record the things that make you feel anxious, discouraged, or unqualified. Include any other negative feeling you may have experienced working towards your career goals.

For every negative emotion or reaction you write in your journal, write three to five *positive* experiences or pieces of information that show that you really *can* overcome this obstacle. These can be incidents when you were praised or rewarded for a skill or trait, or simple pieces of information about your qualifications and accomplishments. You can dig as far back as early childhood or as recent as earlier in the day!

This is an especially great exercise when you are struggling to find positive solutions to challenges. You can also employ this exercise in a group setting; doing so allows you to sample a wider range of insights and possibilities for a business, project, or other challenging undertaking.

PASSION AND PURPOSE TASK 7.2: TRACK YOUR VICTORIES

It's easy to look at the hurdles and boundaries in front of you and feel defeated. It's even easier to look at what seems an endless task and feel like you haven't achieved anything.

Keeping a list of victories can help you reevaluate your accomplishments, where your efforts have gone, and what progress you have made.

Remember, even when you've made progress, your brain may still feel inclined to pay more attention to what you *haven't* completed yet. Don't let it fool you into thinking that your goal is a lion that's going to eat you!

Method to make actionable goals:

1. State the problem clearly
2. Identify the specific strengths and resources you have
3. Design a strategy
4. Create simple, individual action items that need to be completed to implement the strategy
5. Implement the strategy as effectively as possible

Break down tasks or wants into goals. Put them on your calendar. Schedule these tasks. Particularly large challenges or goals should be broken down into multiple milestones.

The smaller and simpler each individual step that you describe is, the easier it will be to get them done. For example, items like "spend an hour researching jobs in this field in my area" requires much less thinking to implement than "find the best jobs to apply to," which is a process that could involve many steps. Breaking it down into individual, concrete actions—actions you need to take—will make it much easier to complete the whole goal.

Check off the steps you complete as you succeed. Remember, every small achievement is a step towards victory! Any time you experience a major success, write it down. Acknowledge this accomplishment. This trains your brain to keep rewarding you with positive emotions. This trains your brain to enjoy success.

PASSION AND PURPOSE TASK 7.3: COUNTERING NEGATIVE BELIEF

Many of us may begin our careers or our job searches with negative beliefs about our goals and ourselves. That is, we may have been taught—by experience, or those around us—that aiming too high is pointless, that we are unlikely to experience success. Similar beliefs may make us feel as if there's no point in even trying to achieve our dreams and goals.

These belief systems often have their roots in the negativity bias we discussed earlier, where the brain tries to make us avoid uncomfortable situations. The problem with that, of course, is that some of the most uncomfortable situations—job applications and interviews—are situations that will bring us success if we pull it together and keep pursuing them!

Perhaps you have had friends or family members who find dream job applications and interviews so uncomfortable that they have given up on them—and encouraged you to do the same. Perhaps you have had negative experiences where people told you were unlikely to succeed, or that there was no point in trying.

Negative beliefs come from many places and most of us enter adulthood with, unfortunately, more than a few of them. We can achieve much more than we have been taught to expect if we can counter the negative beliefs that prevent us from trying and persisting.

For this exercise, write a goal you would like to achieve, but currently seems unattainable to you. To start with, come up with ten things you could do to turn that goal into a reality. As before, the simpler and more specific a step, the better.

These steps can be as simple as researching a question on the internet, getting a friend to practice job interviews with you, or going to a local school or career office to ask about resources.

Now, keep that piece of paper with your goal written on it. Put it somewhere conspicuous—could be your bathroom mirror or bedroom door. At the end of each day, write down *something* you did that was intended to bring you one step closer to your goal.

If you find yourself going to bed without having written anything, you can always do a quick Google search of a career-relevant question, or send a text or e-mail to a potential resource, in order to complete your "homework" for the day. It's amazing how much of a difference the smallest actions contribute to making our goals a reality.

After ten days, you might be amazed by how much more realistic your goal now seems!

If the goal is not achieved at the end of the 10 days, write down what the next steps are for accomplishing this goal and continue.

Success's most important ingredients are your own attitude and effort—but outside circumstances are important, too. An unsafe or hostile workplace can make life difficult, even if the job description and career field are otherwise suitable.

Discrimination is a particularly ugly challenge some of us face. People can face discrimination from employers or coworkers for a variety of reasons—sex, gender identity, race, religion, disability, or family situation.

Employees in some fields can also face challenges from unsafe working conditions; jobs where labor laws are ignored, or employers fail to properly handle dangerous materials.

Fortunately, we live in a country that offers some legal protections for us, to back us up if we encounter obstacles we might feel powerless to tackle alone.

We will discuss resources for tackling discrimination and workplace safety concerns in Chapters 16 and 17 in Part 2. If these concerns are of particular interest to you, feel free to skip ahead now and come back to Chapter 8 after you've taken a look.

KEY TAKEAWAY

Take time regularly to consciously manage your thoughts and beliefs, so that they don't have power over you.

CHAPTER 8
LIFELONG LEARNING

Just as established products and brands need
updating to stay alive and vibrant, you periodically
need to refresh or reinvent yourself.
– Mireille Guiliano

Our world is changing rapidly, with new tools and new ways of doing business emerging seemingly every day. This means that staying up-to-date on the latest developments can give you a competitive edge. It also means that new opportunities are emerging—new careers and work situations that might not have existed even a few years ago.

For that reason, it can be helpful to look at your skills and goals and interrogate those that haven't been updated in the last couple of years. The internet offers us access to countless ways to stay up-to-date— journals and magazines, online and in-person seminars and courses, community center and community college courses, and even blogs that cover the latest developments in a given field.

I had a client, Rosa, who was 71 years old. She did not want to retire, but she could no longer perform the rigorous physical labor her E.R. nursing career required. She found my services online and signed up for a webinar. She wanted help finding her passion and channeling it into a new career. She was especially interested in developing a vocation that would take advantage of her experience while meeting her need for less physical rigor.

She not only gained valuable insight into the patterns woven into her life story, she was able to discern corridors that were open to her as a highly experienced nurse. She also offered mentorship, insight, and wisdom to other clients in the webinar—younger clients in their twenties. This new medium brought people with complementary sets of knowledge and expertise together; who might never have met otherwise!

Rosa was ultimately delighted to take advantage of a recent development, facilitated by new technologies and policies—the field of telemedicine, where nurses and doctors speak with patients and offer basic recommendations via phone or over the internet. She is now able to work from the comfort of her own home as a telemedicine nurse given her tremendous amount of hands-on medical experience.

As people live longer and technology makes for more flexible working arrangements, and remote work positions, work opportunities for older people are increasing. So are opportunities for younger people to achieve greater work/life balance by leveraging technology to obtain flexible work hours, or locations, or to work directly with their own clients as freelancers instead of relying solely on employers for income.

Important developments that might be relevant to your career include:

Technical developments. Today our world is filled with new techniques, discoveries, and technologies that can give you new capabilities if you understand them. In a world of constantly evolving apps and web services, it may be possible to truly wow an employer, client, or potential employer by refreshing your knowledge and periodically looking for new tools.

Job market developments. New types of jobs are constantly being created; certain jobs are becoming less common, salaries are changing. Work culture is also changing, all of which leads to demand for new skills that might give you an edge if you acquire them.

- https://www.MyNextMove.org is an excellent free re-source with lots of data for learning about new job market trends and projections. As you pull together all your inter-ests, patterns, and strengths, consider seeking out resources that will help you stay up-to-date on your skills and knowledge of your target career field. Being able to tell em-ployers that you're up-to-date on the latest techniques and technology, or that you have a skill that can give them a competitive edge, is a definite asset on résumés, cover let-ters, and in interviews.

Government policy changes that affect your career field. For ex-ample, telemedicine positions were quite rare ten years ago, but with rising costs of healthcare, and stricter government requirements com-pelling insurance companies to offer more to their customers, many in-surance companies have begun hiring nurses to speak with customers by phone to provide more cost-effective and accessible health and med-ical advice.

BENEFITS OF LIFELONG LEARNING

Employers always seek the best-qualified candidates, and they often look at how recently you have been trained in a skill. They are also likely to be impressed if you have job-relevant certificates or certifications. If you can show recent certifications, workshops, and newly acquired skills you will assure the prospective employer that you have a lot to contribute—and, just as importantly, that you are dedicated and proac-tive when it comes to being the best you can be at your job.

Lifelong learning is also personally beneficial. You may learn about emerging skills or jobs that are a better fit for your life's goals and values than what you have right now. You may even find yourself in a good position to become a consultant or entrepreneur if you are particularly good at keeping up with industry trends.

Often the biggest hurdle to engaging in new learning is the fear of failure. Just like when applying to jobs, we may be anxious about not performing well on continuing education coursework.

When this happens, we can use the exercises from the last chapter to help us break our tasks down into to-do lists of manageable steps. It may also help to enlist the help of a friend or colleague. Perhaps you know someone who would also benefit from continued education, and you two could be better together by motivating each other and keeping each other accountable!

Once we are engaged, we often find the fears are not realities, and that we enjoy whatever was making us anxious! I have a hard time naming a client who hasn't found that they enjoyed the challenge of continued learning—and the benefits that came with it—once they undertook it.

There is no right or wrong way to receive new training. The list below is some of my favorite places to go to for knowledge and skill training. If you need a degree, certificate, or just the self-confidence, stop procrastinating and go for it.

ONLINE RESOURCES

Google: This may seem obvious, but I've seen many cases where people didn't think to do a simple Google search for a topic or question that was on their mind. Google often has answers to highly specific questions, written by experts in the field. Many experts maintain blogs that can be accessed via Google.

YouTube: Many colleges and universities have online lectures on YouTube for free. If you search the topic you are interested in, you can see what is available to you for free.

Udemy: Udemy is a global learning and teaching marketplace. Students can master new skills and update established ones by buying courses from an extensive library of over 55,000 courses taught by expert instructors. Udemy courses are broken down into short lectures, making them ideal for learners who cannot devote long hours.

EdX.org: Founded by Harvard University and MIT in 2012, edX is an online learning destination and MOOC provider. It offers high-quality courses from the world's best universities and institutions. EdX university members top the QS World University Rankings® with their founders receiving the top honors.

Coursera.org: Coursera provides courses taught by top instructors from the world's best universities and educational institutions. They include recorded video lectures, auto-graded and peer-reviewed assignments, and community discussion forums. When you complete a course, you'll receive a shareable electronic Course Certificate.

khanacademy.org: Khan Academy is a personalized learning resource for all ages, starting to kindergarten and onward. They offer practice exercises, instructional videos, and a personalized learning dashboard. This empower learners to study at their own pace. Subjects include math, science, computer programming, history, art history, economics, and more. Khan Academy has partnered with institutions like NASA, various Museums of Modern Art, The California Academy of Sciences, and MIT to offer specialized content.

Openculture.com: Open Culture, founded in 2006, brings together high-quality cultural & educational media for lifelong learners. Open Culture centralizes online courses, movies, audio, eBooks, and other content for any user all of it free.

Stanford Free Online Adult Courses: The Office of the Vice Provost for Teaching and Learning (VPTL) creates free online courses, graduate and professional certificates, advanced degrees, and executive education programs, facilitated through engagement with Stanford faculty. Activities range from recorded special talks on iTunes to Master's Degree classes.

Federal Services

The Department of Labor's Employment and Training Administration (ETA) can be a great asset as it provides information on training programs and other services for workers who have been, or will be, laid off.

You can visit http://www.CareerOneStop.org/LocalHelp/service-locator.aspx or call toll-free help line at (877) US-2JOBS (TTY: 1-877-889-5267). Services are location based.

The Department of Vocational Rehabilitation: this resource helps provide people who face mental, emotional, or physical challenges to employment by teaching relevant skills.

Conditions that may qualify you for assistance through the Department of Vocational Rehabilitation can include ADHD, anxiety, depression, PTSD, traumatic brain injury, and physical injuries that limit your ability to do certain types of work.

To be accepted by the Department of Vocational Rehabilitation, you must have a doctor confirm that your mental, emotional, or physical condition is a challenge to your obtaining employment.

If you find yourself wondering if you are "disabled enough" to qualify for their assistance, ask yourself: does your condition present an obstacle to finding employment, or to finding employment specifically in the area you are trained for?

If the answer feels to you like "yes," it is probably worth finding a doctor who is willing to do an assessment to help you begin the process of applying for these services. The Department's support can include expert advice, coaching, and paid tuition for certain training programs. Their goal is to help everyone be employed.

If you do qualify for the Department's services, Rehabilitation Counselors will work closely with you to determine an employment goal and identify and arrange for the services that will be needed to achieve this goal.

Vocational Technical Centers: Although for decades the emphasis in America has been on going to a four-year college, there are tens of millions of high-paying jobs that do *not* require a bachelor's degree. Instead, these jobs require specialized, highly technical, and hands-on training—vocational training.

High-paying careers that require technical training instead of a bachelor's degree include truck drivers, cosmetologists (hair stylists and other types of style experts), auto mechanics, electricians, welders, line workers for power companies, oil rig workers, and Information Technology experts such as cybersecurity experts.

Schools that specialize in each of these professions—and many more—can be found on the internet. Some may be attached to community colleges, while others such as trucking, power line work, or oil rigging, may be run directly by employers.

These companies are eager to fill openings with trained workers, and in some cases may even have scholarship or reduced cost tuition programs available for people who are interested in the field, but are concerned about the cost of training to become qualified.

If you are considering a skilled trade, do some research. Identify what degrees or training programs are most valued in your field, and the local or online schools or companies that offer them.

You should be wary of online training programs, however. Some industries do accept some online training, but vocational training usually needs to include a hands-on component to be valuable, and not every online college or course is well-respected. It's worth taking the time to research the credentials employers in the field like—including what schools or training programs are their favorites—before signing up for any online courses.

Community Resources
Colleges:

Most colleges offer online courses for which you can receive credit. They may also allow enrollment in in-person courses on an as-needed basis instead of as a full-time student. These can be helpful if you are trying to work towards a degree or certificate.

If you are a student currently, your college probably has a Career Center that offers employment skills assistance—directories of resources for careers and jobs in your field, as well as cover letter, résumé, and interviewing tips and assistance.

Community Centers:

Community Centers are organizations, often funded by government grants, that help people gain skills, knowledge, and find opportunities for business and employment. These centers are most common in urban areas but may also be found in smaller cities or towns.

Services commonly offered by Community Centers include résumé and cover letter assistance, job training resources, and networking opportunities. Think of Community Centers as you would a college's Career Center. The only difference is they serve all taxpayers, including non-student workers and businesspeople. Community Centers often offer services specifically for people who speak English as a Second Language and are eager to help people who are new to English put their job skills and education to use.

Apprenticeships:

An apprenticeship is a training system in which a newcomer to a career field assists an experienced worker in that field, and rapidly gains expertise and experience in the process.

Apprenticeships are not as common as they once were, but it is sometimes possible to *create* an apprenticeship opportunity, if you are sufficiently enthusiastic about the career field, and are able to form a personal connection with an expert.

Experts and business owners are often eager to have assistants who are highly motivated to learn all aspects of the trade or business. For them, having a new employee who is eager to learn exactly how they do things might be preferable to trying to hire regular employees who may or may not be interested in learning and taking on more responsibilities over time.

It is important to note that unlike internships, apprenticeships are regulated by the federal government. While internships are often very brief and unpaid, or "paid in experience," under the Apprenticeship Act employers must pay apprentices a monthly stipend. Apprenticeships usually last for 6 months to a year.

Apprenticeship stipends are sometimes not enough to live on, so it may be important to have savings or a second job while working in an apprenticeship. However, apprenticeships are a great foot in the door into an industry, and are often less expensive and more valued by employers than simply taking classes on a subject.

If you've decided you may like to get work experience and a foot in the door in a new industry through an apprenticeship, here are some steps you can follow to create an apprenticeship opportunity for yourself:

1. Research: Find the trade or job you are most interested in and start research. Look for industry trends, salary potential, cultural climate etc. It may be helpful to reread the information you collected in Part I of this book to ensure you are directing your interests to a career path that will work for you.

2. Informational or mentorship interview: Reach out to people in the field and let them know you are interested in entering. The best people to approach are people whose career you think you

may someday wish to have. They can tell you answers to questions like how they got to where they are, and who the best people in the industry to train under are. We will talk more about informational, or mentorship interviewing in Part II.

It is a good idea to prepare an "elevator pitch" about why you think your skills and personality are particularly well-suited to this field, and why you are passionate about it. Potential mentors or contacts know that the more passionate and self-aware a student is, the easier they are to teach.

With the help of experts in the field, you can learn the answers to important questions such as:

- If the mentor has your dream job, how did they get to where they are today?
- What would be the best job for you to pursue, given your personality and interests?
- What would be the best place for you to start pursuing that job, as an apprentice, student, or entry-level worker?
- What specific skills would you need to do that job well?
- What kind of training would you need?
    o Identify companies that are apprentice-friendly.
- Apprenticeship.gov is a website run by the Department of Labor. It has information to help you find existing apprenticeship opportunities near you, learn more about creating apprenticeships,
- You may also wish to inquire with companies you know you'd like to work for about whether they are interested in taking on an apprentice with your combination of passion, personality, skills, achievements, and experiences.
- Apprenticeship.gov includes information about how apprenticeships benefit businesses, and how to start one. That might be useful for you to know when you are opening a

discussion with a company about whether they would be interested in taking you on as an apprentice.

- o Always read the fine print. It's common for people who are new to an industry to sign a contract that is not a good deal for them, because they are not familiar with what to watch out for or ask. They are often taught to do what the employer says, so may sign contracts assuming they are good.
- If possible, it may benefit you to have an independent mentor figure in the field, or a lawyer if one is available, look over any contract before you sign it to be sure the terms are favorable to you.

If a contract is not favorable to you, you can always make line edits and ask the employer if the terms you are supplying would work for them instead.

Negotiating contracts is an art—it is about coming to the most beneficial agreement for both parties, and learning what is important to each one.

With the information contained here, you are well-equipped to know what kinds of opportunities exist, and where to find them. This information is very useful, whether you're about to graduate from high school or making a midlife career change.

KEY TAKEAWAY

Lifelong learning keeps you in touch with are rapidly changing society and keeps you active, happy, and positively challenged.

CHAPTER 9
SELF-CARE

Self-care is how you take your power back.
– Lalah Delia

Self-care is not often discussed in career books. Traditionally, the thinking has been that taking care of oneself is a private activity that belongs at home.

But as psychological science advances, scientists are realizing that many people, like my client Tara, have great, untapped career potential that they are not using because they have not learned how to care for their personal needs and work with the strengths they have.

In this chapter, I'll share some examples of how caring for yourself and recognizing your needs can help you to be more effective in the workplace, and in fulfilling your personal purpose. To make it easier to see which approaches might be helpful to you, I'll list example solutions based on challenges you might face.

At first glance, these lists might seem overwhelming—I propose a lot of self-care measures. Try taking the two or three self-care measures from each section that feel most relevant to you and build a schedule for daily or weekly self-care. You can also use these to form a "protocol" for what to do when you feel challenges arising.

Even as a hypothetical exercise, it will likely be very interesting to see how you might be able to incorporate these measures into your life. It might even be worth an experiment to see how well they work.

WHEN YOU ARE OVERWHELMED

In recent years, mental illness diagnoses have been on the rise. Perhaps due to our society's increasingly complex demands, many people now experience, at least, temporary depression, which can manifest symptoms including obvious ones like sadness and hopelessness, but also feelings of fatigue, low motivation, procrastination, and chronic frustration.

Many people lose sight of the fact that our bodies are our vehicles in life. We are often taught to approach problems intellectually, and to view our health and physical maintenance as things that don't require much attention.

But the obvious truth is, our bodies are intimately involved in determining our mood and the biochemical environment of our brain. As such, neglecting our body's needs over time—something that is particularly easy to do when we are feeling hopeless, fatigued, unmotivated, or overwhelmed by school or career demands—can lead to biochemical imbalances.

When clients come to me, they often feel a little bit overwhelmed by the demands of school or work, or depressed that they have not made the career progress they want despite their best efforts.

In addition to learning and strategizing about their personalities and available career options, I often recommend that they identify and come up with plans to address some of their body's needs, too.

Examples
Earlier in this book, we talked about Brad—a computer scientist who found he was unhappy working with just machines for his company all day.

Brad struggled with depression like almost all isolated extraverts.

Depression can make it especially challenging to take care of yourself, let alone make career changes. Although he was working hard to do those things, it was much harder for him than he might have liked.

After talking to Brad, I suspected that his diet might hold part of the answer. In his depression he had not been eating a balanced diet, and he sometimes found it to be a struggle to prepare healthy meals. We also discovered that Brad felt best when he was physically moving around—probably one reason why sitting in a room full of computers all day wasn't working for him.

I made a few recommendations for Brad, to help him feel good and give his body what it needed, even when he was lacking the energy to cook a healthy meal or go to the gym.

To discover what types of self-care you could benefit from, ask yourself:

Are you an introvert or an extravert?
Different things may exhaust different people. Brad was exhausted by not having enough human contact in his isolating job—but others may be exhausted by having too *much* social contact in their job, or in their personal life.

Sometimes prioritizing "me time"—whether that means spending time alone, or with friends—can help you to recover from a job that doesn't give you what you need to stay energized.

Are you sleeping enough?
In today's competitive world, some people use the motto, "sleep is for the weak." The opposite is true!

The brain and body perform many essential maintenance functions during sleep. Fatigue, impaired learning ability, impaired cognitive performance, impaired ability to focus, and feelings of frustration and irritability are common side effects of not getting enough sleep. Sleep deprivation can even lead to illness, since the immune system and the hormones that modulate blood sugar, blood pressure, and healing responses are also regulated during sleep.

So even if it feels like you have a lot to do, one of the most important tasks has to be sleep. Many fitness watches track your sleep cycle now. Sleep works to improve your mood, cognitive performance, and physical health.

Is the food you eat energizing you?

We decided that Brad would benefit from creating a meal plan. By devoting one afternoon per week to shopping and preparing meals and ingredients, we could take much of the daily burden of meal prep and healthy eating off his plate. With proper organization, shopping, prep, and cooking were taken care of all in one day. So for the rest of the week Brad could simply grab ready-to-eat meals and ingredients from his fridge when he got hungry. For the extra busy person a meal delivery service might be a solution that ensures nutritious meals are prepared.

With some clients, I even encourage setting phone alarms to make sure that they eat *something* on a regular basis. Even if it feels like a chore, giving your brain the fuel it needs to function properly can improve your mood, energy levels, and performance.

If you struggle with eating or cooking, would it help to develop a preparation system that could make it simple for you to assemble healthy meals, or just grab them out of the fridge?

Are there herbs or vitamins that could help?

Brad also decided to try taking a nervous system support supplement that was available through a Natural Grocers in his area. Many supplements and vitamin blends are available to help supply the ingredients your brain needs to make the neurotransmitters that give you energy and pleasure.

Are you consuming a lot of energy-sapping ingredients like sugar, caffeine, and sodium?

Many people with demanding jobs drink a great deal of caffeine to keep them alert and energized. However, too much caffeine can interfere with sleep and other natural processes that your body needs to become truly refreshed. If you are masking symptoms of stress and fatigue with a temporary caffeine hit, and doing this for long periods of time, your body ends up with a lot of built-up fatigue!

Many people also eat large amounts of sugar or salt, because comfort food and pre-packaged, no-prep snacks tend to have large quantities of these flavoring ingredients. The problem is this can also affect your body's energy levels and neurological functioning. Eating large amounts of sugar can disrupt your body's ability to ensure that constant levels of fuel are available for your cells. Salt is involved in nervous system activity, including nerves that control stress responses.

Purchasing, preparing, and packing healthy, unprocessed foods to take with you to work or school can make a big difference to how you feel and what you are able to accomplish.

Are you moving around enough?

We also decided that Brad could use some reason—any reason—to go outside and get moving every day. As it happened, he had a neighbor whose dog needed daily walks. Brad arranged with his neighbor to walk the dog every day after he got home from work. Having another living being waiting eagerly for him to exercise each evening helped tremendously with Brad's motivation and offered a low-stress form of exercise.

Physical exercise and time spent in nature are both scientifically shown to improve mood and energy levels. Going to the gym, yoga classes, jogging, or spending time in with plants or natural bodies of water have all been shown to have concrete, positive effects on our mood and biochemistry. This effect is so powerful that some hospitals are now creating large indoor gardens with small streams or ponds in them to help their patients heal faster.

The measures that motivate you, and are accessible to you, may vary from person to person. But if you are struggling with low energy or symptoms of depression, try incorporating one of the measures into your daily or weekly routine and see how you feel.

If moving around motivates you, is there a simple and fun way that you could commit to spending some time moving every day? Ask your doctor. That is always an excellent resource in this situation.

In Brad's case, his feelings of depression, low energy, and low motivation were caused by a career that deprived him of an important means of getting energy for someone with his personality. But there are also medical conditions that can cause low energy and depression due to strictly internal biochemical changes, which may not go away without medication.

So if you have been feeling low-energy or depressed for several months, it is a good idea to discuss your symptoms with a doctor. They may be able to order biochemical tests or prescribe medications that can really help.

By battling his depression, Brad was able to do the necessary work to move into a job where he thrived. Remember, depression can make positive change feel impossible—and if you are suffering from depression, it is well-worth devoting time and energy to discovering what energizes you, and how to fit that into your daily routine.

WHEN YOU HAVE TROUBLE FOCUSING

As scientific research progresses, scientists are increasingly realizing that our 40-hour work week may not be very well-designed. Studies have shown that employee productivity drops when people are cooped up at desks, or in another monotonous environment, for many hours at a time. This productivity can look like trouble concentrating, tiredness, or simply making mistakes, or feeling unable to get work done for no clear reason.

My clients are neuro-diverse—some suffer from chronic illness or injuries; some have emotional or psychological challenges. These conditions can create especially acute difficulty with concentrating or performing for long periods of time.

But most of you have probably noticed some degree of difficulty with "the 2:30 slump," or simply being "off your game."

In this section, we'll talk about strategies I recommend for my clients with cognitive challenges that can also help anyone.

My client Tara was particularly prone to brain fog and difficulty concentrating because of her dual challenges, ADHD and traumatic brain injury. When her brain was working well, she did incredibly good work, but her brain would often simply refuse to focus on the task at hand. Here are some strategies we developed together to help her perform when she needed to and secure her dream job:

WHAT HELPS YOU "RESET?"

Tara found that physical movement and changes of scenery both helped her brain to "refresh" or "reset." This is in keeping with scientific findings that meetings and offices which incorporate "walking" into their routines see measurably higher productivity.

To take advantage of this effect, Tara developed a routine that she would use right before she needed to deliver a big speech or presentation, or in the middle of the day if she was simply feeling foggy.

Before big presentations or decisions, Tara would go outside and spend fifteen minutes walking around the block. To avoid going on "autopilot" and seeing this as simply one more job duty, she would switch up her route so that she saw different parts of the neighborhood on each walk. Sometimes she would even do "penny walks," where she flipped a coin to decide which way to go at corners and intersections, in order to keep herself in the moment.

Tara found that walking, having physical activity away from the scrutiny of coworkers, helped her brain to process information and allowed her to tackle the task at hand much more effectively when she got back to the office.

Some employers may not be enthusiastic about employees taking time away from the desk, but if you feel this measure might help you to "reset" and improve your performance, there are scientific studies you can cite which might convince your employer that it's worth an experiment to see how taking walks affects your productivity.

A simple Internet search for phrases such as "taking walks improves worker productivity" will turn up a plethora of the latest articles about research on the subject.

TAKE TIME TO PRACTICE NOT THINKING.

Tara also began a ten-minute meditation practice at the beginning of the day. Many of the world's most successful people recommend ten minutes of meditation, at least once a day, as a means of stepping back from stress and focusing on long-term goals.

The true experts—the world's most successful people—recommend ten minutes of meditation three times a day as a routine—first thing in the morning, at noon around lunchtime, and then at night before bed. But meditation sessions can also be used as-needed at your desk, in the break room, or on your walks, to clear your mind, let go of stress, and remind yourself of your goal.

Just like taking fifteen-minute walks, ten-minute meditation sessions can be used any time they feel useful, such as when stress threatens to overwhelm.

What could you gain from taking ten minutes a few times a day to simply breathe, clear your mind, and remember why you're doing what you're doing?

Could you benefit from tapping?

One easy-to-use therapeutic technique that is especially beneficial for people who have anxiety, chronic pain, or trouble focusing is "tapping."

There are a plethora of YouTube videos describing different tapping techniques. Different tapping techniques may be especially useful for certain conditions. The principle is that simply by tapping on certain parts of your body with your fingers, you can change and refocus your brain activity.

This makes sense. The brain tends to focus on new or acute stimuli, and physical sensations like tapping definitely count. There is also some evidence for the idea that stimulating acupuncture/acupressure points change brain and body processes in ways that scientists don't fully understand.

Not much scientific research has been done on tapping; it is a fairly new technique. Some scientists caution that claims about benefits made by businesses that sell tapping instruction and techniques might be exaggerated.

But free, basic tapping tutorials can be found online. It's free to try, and some people with anxiety, chronic pain, or trouble focusing do report benefits from tapping. Anything that benefits you is a tool worth having in your career goal toolbox!

Have you explored the Joy of Missing Out?

The Joy of Missing Out—or JOMO—is a new idea. As you might have guessed, it is the opposite of Fear of Missing Out, or FOMO.

Where FOMO is anxiety brought on by social media, which shows us more events, accomplishments, and conversations than we can possibly participate in each day, leaving many people feeling left-out, JOMO, is the joy that we obtain by intentionally stepping back from what everyone else is doing to enjoy and focus on our own lives.

JOMO may include declining social invitations to dedicate time to self-care, or simply turning off one's phone for a set amount of time, or for one day each week. Some people go so far as to do an "Internet fast" where they physically switch off their router for a set amount of time so they cannot be tempted to look at social media.

JOMO measures that allow you to be isolated from outside demands and influences set an excellent stage for some sleep, relaxation, meditation, reading, or spending time in nature.

Know your limits

For people with chronic illnesses or injuries, pushing yourself past your limits can be disastrous. Tara, for example, could suffer from days of fatigue or brain fog where she was not able to work if she overwhelmed her nervous system trying to meet employer demands or complete a project.

Brain fog—a condition where a person is unable to concentrate on a task, solve problems, or recall information—is a common ailment that can be brought on by stress, lack of sleep, physical factors such as poor diet, and many medical conditions. While people like Tara who have histories of brain injury must be especially careful not to overtax themselves and cause an episode of brain fog, all brains can experience this kind of impaired functioning as a result of overwork.

Burnout—a long-lasting period of sensitivity to stress and impaired performance—is another possible response to pushing oneself too far for an extended period of time. Burnout can impair one's cognitive and emotional ability to do their job for weeks or months. This can have devastating consequences for one's career.

It is clear that, to reach long-term goals, we must balance ambition with sustainability. Cheetahs are the fastest land animals in the animal kingdom, able to run up to 75 miles per hour. But the cost of their speed is so high that they can only run for about ninety seconds at a time. For this reason, human hunters can chase cheetahs down on foot and hunt them. Cheetahs are capable of amazing bursts of speed, but humans with our more modest speed are capable of more endurance.

So when you are deciding whether to prioritize self-care measures, or spend all your time working or studying, remember—a slower, steadier pace truly does win the race. You will make better decisions, perform better, and enjoy a higher quality of life in the long run, if you take time out to give your brain and body the fuel, rest, and space they need to function at peak performance!

KEY TAKEAWAY

A slower, steadier pace really does win the race. You will have greater long-term success if you learn to support your performance with time scheduled for self-care.

PART II

SUPERCHARGE YOUR JOB HUNT

INTRODUCTION

Change is the law of life. And those who look only to the past or
present are certain to miss the future.
– John F. Kennedy

OPPORTUNITIES IN A CHANGING LABOR MARKET

With the advancement of AI, robotics, and other forms of automation, many people are worried that our economy might soon shed jobs people depend on.

However, for those who are proactive, there are a growing array of remarkable opportunities available because of advancing science and technology.

Corporate Culture

For those who may feel daunted by traditional workplaces with collared shirts and cubicles, changes in corporate culture may prove exciting. Many companies are challenging old assumptions about what constitutes "professional" behavior, and experimenting to see if flexible hours, dress codes, remote work-from-home options, and unusual employee perks produce higher productivity.

In the tech industry in particular, offices often feature less than formal dress codes, and more flexible corporate cultures, where activities like taking walks and meditation breaks may be recognized as part of an employees' optimal workflow. Seeing the success of this approach in tech, companies in other industries are beginning to become open to the idea that a more "human" approach may increase innovation and efficiency.

As technology increases the ability to work collaboratively at a distance, some companies are also experimenting with the idea that it's better to have the right employee—even if that employee isn't local. Some applicants have been able to successfully negotiate remote work positions with the companies of their choice, in order to work from home or avoid relocating to a new city.

Freelancing and Contract Gigs

The Internet and money transfer technology have made it easier than ever before for workers to contract directly with clients, instead of going through a corporate system.

This type of work can afford even greater flexibility, allowing freelancers to choose their own clients, set their own pay rates, and work wherever and whenever they wish. An entire subculture of "digital nomads" who travel the world while supporting themselves with remote freelance work has appeared in recent years.

There are certainly pros and cons to this lifestyle. Job security is low because clients can cancel contracts at any time, and the freelance worker does all the work of finding clients and gigs themselves. Freelancers are also solely responsible for paying for their own medical care, saving for retirement, and acquiring other benefits and protections. Without an employer to negotiate contracts or enforce deadlines, high-caliber negotiating skills and self-discipline are necessary to good outcomes.

However, for people with lots of self-discipline and keen negotiating skills who value flexibility and freedom, the growing gig economy provides more opportunities than ever before to turn a steady income while making one's own decisions about one's work environment and schedule. The gig economy may be especially helpful for people who aspire to travel the world before settling down, or those who wish to have a career while also being a stay-at-home parent or caregiver.

Social Consciousness

Social Consciousness in business is the idea of striving to make a positive impact on your community, or on the world, with your business. With growing information about the interconnectedness of businesses with community, and many consumers giving preference to socially conscious organizations, Corporate Social Responsibility (CSR) is becoming a larger concern for employers.

This has allowed many socially conscious entrepreneurs to enter the corporate world in the fields of PR, social media, and sustainability, or to create their own businesses to fill an under-served social responsibility niche.

Staying On-Track

You may wish to consider whether teaming up with a friend who also seeks to forward their career might help motivate you to reach your goals.

The power of partnership can push us to succeed in ways we never would have done if we were working on our own. Perhaps in this way, you and a friend can both reap the fruits of creating proactive life habits and careers for yourselves.

CHAPTER 10
STARTING YOUR JOB SEARCH

Some people dream of success, while other people get up every morning and make it happen.

– Wayne Huizenga

Most people find job hunting to be a stressful experience. Many who have not searched for jobs before, or lately, don't know where to even begin. Having a game plan for how to start can help you stay on track and give you tangible goals to check off.

Most people will likely want to dive right into applying for the first appealing job available. But taking some time to consider what you really want and need in a job, and compiling a list of potential jobs to compare, will increase the chances that you find the ideal fit for you. Remember, you only need one job. It is better to conduct thorough research and identify what's available, as opposed to pursuing the first merely 'acceptable' job you see.

Try going through the questions below before you start sending out job applications:

KNOWING WHAT YOU WANT

1. **What kind of job are you looking for?**
    Take time to think about what you've learned about yourself.
    How do your interests fit into the kind of job you desire? What
    kind of daily job duties should this job have, or what kinds of
    duties should it avoid? Visualize this job and describe it.

2. **Now think about the skills you have identified and see how
    they fit into this type of career.**
    What skills do you have that would make you especially good
    at it? Do you have any weak skills that might pose a problem
    with the job description?

3. **Visualize your ideal workplace.** What kind of people do you
    need to work with? What does it look and feel like? Describe it
    here.

4. **How much money do you need to make?** Do you want to
    prioritize the highest-paying jobs, or would you rather have a
    career that matches your desires in other ways than a high-earn-
    ing one?
    Think of your expenses, ambitions, and lifestyle. What would
    it take to realistically live like this?

5. **What types of duties, responsibilities, and schedule do you
    feel that you would like to have in the new job?** Think about
    your skills, self-care findings, work habits, and dreams of the
    perfect job.

6. **Now, list five steps you will take to find this job.**

Will you search online job boards? Compare postings you find there?
Customize your résumé for each individual job, to emphasize the
strengths and accomplishments which fit that particular organization?

MAKING THE ACTION PLAN

Anyone can *say* they want to achieve something, but I'm sure you've experienced how actually achieving goals we set can be challenging. We're much more likely to succeed if we create an action plan that is SMART.

You might think your goals are plenty smart—but here, SMART is an acronym for a goal that will definitely be accomplished if you follow through with your plans.

A SMART goal has the attributes that follow, making it highly achievable:

Specific. Your goal should state, concretely, exactly what outcome you are trying to achieve. Is it the completion of a certain to-do list? A certain number of hours per week devoted to an activity? A certain number of jobs applied for?

Measurable. It should be possible to measure with certainty whether you have achieved your goal. Measurements could include the checking off of items on a to-do list, the tracking of hours per week devoted to your task, or the tracking of how many jobs you have applied for.

Achievable. Your goal should be something you know you can attain. For example, you may not be able to guarantee that you will get a certain number of job offers in a certain frame of time, because you don't have control over how employers operate. But you can definitely achieve a certain number of job offers sent out, or a certain amount of time devoted to interview practice.

Relevant. This may seem obvious, but your SMART goal should directly assist you to reach your big goals—the most important goals in your life. The more relevant, the better—perhaps you want to not just apply to a certain *number* of jobs, but ensure that these are jobs that meet a certain number of your "ideal job" criteria.

Time-bound. This means you give yourself a deadline. A SMART goal will not take you where you want to go very fast, if you keep telling yourself you'll get to it next month. Set weekly, monthly, or quarterly SMART goals. If you haven't achieved your SMART goals by their due dates, figure out why, and how you can overcome that obstacle.

It is not uncommon for someone to say, "I want to get a job I like," and consider that a goal. A SMART approach may break down this process into job-identification, preparation, application, and interviewing goals. In this way, each goal consists of concrete and immediate actions you can take, rather than a nebulous outcome like "find a job."

How will you define "a job you like?" What specific steps do you need to take? Drill all the way down. List individual actions like "make a list of things I want in a job," "identify ten possible candidate jobs," and "apply to each of those jobs."

As you look through your opportunities, you may be overwhelmed by your options. Consider keeping this list and your SMART goal close at hand.

That way you always have a highly specific list of small steps you can take, one at a time, to find your way into the best job for you.

CHAPTER 11
KNOW WHAT EMPLOYERS WANT

Our chief want is someone who will inspire us
to be what we know we could be.
– Ralph Waldo Emerson

In any negotiation, your strength lies in being able to offer the other party what they want. If you know their business or their clientele very well, you may even be able to offer things they didn't *know* they wanted until you brought it to the table.

The task of helping employers realize that *you* are what they want is made more complicated by the fact that employers tend to hire people they already know, instead of looking to the wider public for the perfect applicant.

As this book goes on, we'll show you how to use that principle to your advantage by:

1. Cultivating mentorship relationships with star players in your industry.
2. Using your social and professional network to connect with people inside businesses that may be seeking to fill positions.

GETTING AN IN

The best way to become eligible for inside positions *before* positions are posted to the public is to choose companies you know you'd like to work for and approach them through anyone you may know (or have something in common with) who works in a decision-making capacity at the company. This subset of people you know are commonly referred to as *"referrals," "your contacts,"* or *"bridge people."* Your referrals or bridge people can be former classmates, former colleagues, friends, friends-of-friends, or people you find via social or professional networking sites. In general, the better a referral knows you, the more effective they will be at promoting you to the company. Contacts may not be very enthusiastic about recommending people they've only met through LinkedIn, but if you are a close friend of someone at the company, or a close friend of a close friend, they will be more motivated to keep you in mind as a potential future hire.

There are many ways to expand one's number of contacts. These include industry conventions, where people with common career interests from many different companies go to learn new skills and socialize. There is also Meetup.com, a website that hosts groups for professionals in your industry and city. The last place to expand your contacts of course are parties thrown by friends who work or study in your area of interest.

Some Meetup.com professional networking groups exist in most cities and towns, but these and other options can be difficult for those with transportation challenges. This makes online networking sites—such as LinkedIn—very useful. When you find a company where you'd like to work, you should search all of your online contacts to determine if anyone you know has any inside contacts.

You can also reach out and offer your services directly to people who work at the company, though this has a somewhat lower chance of success if the people you are reaching out to have never heard of you before. Getting inside contacts allows you to have few if any competitors, because companies may reach out to people they already know before announcing a vacancy to the general public. When you respond to a job post, on the other hand, you can have hundreds competing with you for that one job.

When contacting someone to serve as a bridge person, it's helpful to specify a few things; that way you help them understand what you can offer their company:

Your specific interest in, or enthusiasm for, the company.

Employers know that people who are proactive in seeking out their favorite companies are also likely to be proactive employees serving the company's best interests. When offering your skills, tell your contact person why you are reaching out to this particular company, and why you want to support the company's mission. A company's mission statement can usually be found on its website.

The skills you have been honing that you can use for the company.

It is often helpful to come up with a list of at least three skills, knowledge bases, or accomplishments for your "elevator pitch." You want to be able to show how you could be of unique service to the company.

These skills should cover the basics of a job description you want (i.e. if you are a writer, you should address your writing skill), but may also include any "bonus" background interests, knowledge, skills, achievements, or hobbies that you think the company as a whole could benefit from.

Why you are reaching out to them now.

Did you just complete a degree program or a new certification? Are you switching careers because you've realized some of your skills are underutilized in your current career? Have you been with the same employer for several years, and are now looking to put the skills you've acquired to use in a more expansive position?

Most companies never actually advertise an open position until all other measures have failed.

Still, one can find millions of jobs posted online. Many employers are unable to sufficiently fill open positions through internal hiring. We will discuss how to apply to those in a later chapter.

If you'd like to take additional tests or use additional exercises in an effort gain insight into what you have to offer employers, or which careers have the most to offer you, check out these further resources below.

Suggested Resources for Further Exploration

One of the best online self-inventory programs I have found is www.eParachute.com. My clients find it much more accurate than similar instruments. For example, a client who was a web specialist was given the recommendation "Graphic Design" from eParachute. A different test had recommended she become an accountant!

For those who prefer something in book form instead, I recommend "The Flower Exercise" found in *What Color Is Your Parachute?* and *The Job-Hunters' Workbook* from Ask a Headhunter.

Where to Start Looking

Staffing Agencies
A simple Internet search for staffing agencies in your city will give you access to organizations that will take your résumé and help you find jobs that fit your experience.

Job Boards
Many online job boards are only click of the mouse away. Some of these also have helpful features like company reviews—where current or former employees of a company can leave public reviews of the company's work culture, benefits, and more.

Some of the most popular job search sites are listed below:

Indeed
Glassdoor
CareerBuilder
TheLadders
Monster
SimplyHired
Us.jobs
Zip recruiter

Hansens' Quintessential Careers
A few that are a little off the beaten path:

The Undercover Recruiter — Undercover Recruiter lists some of the best available openings from various online job boards.

Job Crank — the original job-board dedicated to small businesses. Though its primary intent is to list vacancies, you can find the names of many small businesses which may be expanding.

Tap into your networks, ask friends, family, ex-coworkers, anyone, because everyone knows someone.

Craigslist Job Search — Craigslist has something of a mixed reputation, but posts hundreds of legitimate job posts daily. Be particularly careful about scams and do not trust any company that asks you to pay out of pocket for equipment they will later reimburse you for. Be equally suspicious of any company that has strange requirements.

Job Board Reviews — If you find using certain job board sites difficult, this site has users evaluate job boards themselves.

Networking
Meeting people in your field, or your clients' field, is the first step to becoming an insider. There are many places to meet people in your field in a social setting to cultivate long-term relationships, including:

Former Classmates — If your college has an Alumni Association this may prove to be an invaluable resource. Colleges often want to boast about their successful graduates. If you have a stack of business cards, email lists from old addresses you rarely use, or even a rolodex, start looking through names and see where people are now.

Industry Conferences and Events — Many industries have conferences and local events where industry updates, tips, and tricks are shared. These are an excellent way to meet people who are active in your industry. You can often find these events through industry newsletters, your district's Chamber of Commerce, individual organizations, and even Facebook.

Of note: Be wary of industry conferences or events that demand thousands of dollars just to attend, *especially* if they invite you to present as a panelist or "expert" in the field even though you are new to it.

A number of organizations throw fake professional conferences. They profit by demanding high prices for admission without recruiting any actual experts in the field to present useful information. Reputable companies are usually aware of these organizations and will not send employees or representatives to their events. So in addition to being expensive, these fake professional conferences are not good places to network.

Job Fairs — Many job fairs are advertised by workforce agencies, and often federally funded. Visit any local workforce agency in any incorporated town.

Cold Calling — It is possible to 'cold call' a company. That means contacting a company to offer your services without seeing a job ad or being invited by an inside contact. Should you decide to take that step, try not to call on a Friday afternoon or on Monday mornings. Tuesdays are usually best for this.

The best person to contact is a person in a secretarial role who is aware of what's going on and willing to share information about what the company is looking for. While it may be tempting to contact the company's executives directly, they are often too busy to assist job-seekers. It's better to collect information from support staff and learn all you can before seeking to speak with your possible future boss. Practice speaking with authority. Avoid sounding timid or unsure. Remember: you are *offering* them your skills and expertise, not *asking for* a job.

Delphi Forums — Delphi is a member-managed online community that enables individuals to build, manage, and grow.

LinkedIn — LinkedIn lets you collect a network of professional contacts via friends, acquaintances, and their contacts. You can find employees, industry experts, and jobs.

Meetup — This site helps people get together with a group of neighbors who share a common interest. Many towns and cities have a networking club for local businesspeople, or social groups for professionals in different industries.

MyWorkster.com — This networking site builds exclusive, professional college networks, allowing members to get connected to exclusive career opportunities.

NetParty — Netparty is an entry point to networks of professional parties in their 20's and 30's. These events are held at stylish clubs and are meant to be social as well as professional.

Other Resources:
Headhunters — Headhunters are often fee-based, and so may not be the most cost-effective method, but can be helpful for people looking for very specific work for large corporations.

ZoomInfo.com — Zoominfo is a business-information search engine. It provides access to industry information, companies, people, products, services and jobs. You can post/edit a free profile with career details, bio, education, affiliations, contact information, and references.

SOCIAL MEDIA MANAGEMENT

Having a social media presence is more important for people in some industries than others. If your desired career is one that requires public relations, performance, marketing, selling, or influencing the public, having a strong social media presence is a good way to demonstrate your abilities to companies or clients who might search for information about you online.

If your skill set is not directly about selling, but is something the general public might buy, such as a skilled trade or service, having a social media presence that revolves around your trade can help demonstrate your passion and dedication for the field, but is probably not essential.

For example, someone who has a YouTube channel where they make DIY plumbing videos has demonstrated an unusual degree of passion and expertise for the field, but plumbing is not usually a field where social media skills are essential to the job. It is unlikely that most plumbing-related employers are actively looking for future employees on social media.

If you decide to create a social media presence to show off your career-related passion and skill, or if you already have one, here are some tools that can help you:

BranchOut — This application takes your Facebook account to a more professional level, which allows job-seekers to use their personal and professional contacts to find job leads at no cost.

Hootsuite — a leading social media dashboard that lets you manage your Facebook, Twitter, Instagram, LinkedIn and other social media all in one place.

RockMelt — an add-on for your browser, with which you can manage your Facebook, Twitter, YouTube, Tumblr, Gmail, and other accounts.

ListTool — a program that allows users to subscribe, unsubscribe and send commands to mailing and discussion lists.

Jobs with Friends – This resource collects your friends on Facebook and all your links on LinkedIn, and lists them and where they work.

A Note on Social Media
If you have a personal social media account such as Facebook, Twitter, or Instagram, be sure to keep them professional and clean.

This doesn't mean you can't post anything outside of work information, but it does mean you shouldn't post anything that an employer would consider a fireable offense or undesirable employee conduct. Some examples of things that could hurt an employer's opinion of you on social media include:

- Publicly complaining about your current employer or school program. Even if they are problematic, seeing someone publicly complaining about their last job while job hunting can make employers wonder if you are a problem employee, or if you are difficult to please.
- Posting publicly about breaking the rules or lying to your current job or school program. It is surprising how many people do this, and expect not to get caught!
- Posting publicly about legal, financial, or relationship troubles. Fair or not, employers may decide that someone who experiences a lot of distress in these areas may not have enough self-control, financial, or people, skills to be a good team member.
- Posting about excessive drug or alcohol use. Instagramming an occasional glass of wine is no problem, but posts about getting falling-down drunk or jokes about drinking excessively likely only serve to make you an unattractive candidate.

NETWORKING

Networking has changed tremendously in the past two decades thanks to the internet and social media. The changes have also created some unique hurdles. Those who are uncomfortable with online communication can feel as if they are now out of the loop, while those who have never known a time without Facebook may find bridging an online avatar into a professional connection daunting.

Some tips to start connecting or reconnecting:
A LinkedIn study showed that 56% of those who fell into the Millennial age group were introduced to a new job by what started off as casual conversation. If this is true, keeping up with old contacts—even only online—is absolutely worth the time!

If you aren't sure how to start a conversation with someone you haven't spoken to in a while, consider these ideas:

- Start with mentioning how you got connected in the first place.
- Mention something you have in common.
- Comment on something interesting they've done recently.
- Show genuine interest. Remember, everyone has something to teach us!

Once you establish some rapport, start making a list of questions and keep it handy. You want to be ready when things are convenient for them; that could be a month after you break the question or it could be right then and there.

Some conversation starters:

- What has intrigued you about this person's career or something they've mentioned?
- Overlaps in the field?
- What are you most concerned about?

- What are you most excited about?
- What are they most concerned/excited about?

Do *not*, however ask the person directly for a job. If things feel good either ask for a referral to interview, or ask whether they know if the company, or people in the field, are hiring.

Keep in contact after your initial reaching out. No one wants to feel like a mere social convenience. Moreover, if you do end up in the same field, or company, it will be good to have an acquaintance or friend there.

The Elevator Pitch

An elevator pitch is a short, compelling narrative that communicates who you are, what you do, and why you stand out. The term 'elevator pitch' originated because it was meant to be a short explanation of yourself or your work that you could deliver if you should ever find yourself on a brief elevator ride with an important person who you wouldn't otherwise have the opportunity to speak with.

You want to define in one sentence who you are and what you do; your own personal mission statement. Follow that by identifying who, ideally, you'd like to work for. And then a little more about what makes you unique and different. Wrap it up by planting an image of what you'd like to see happen when this is achieved.

Practice your elevator pitch until it rolls naturally off your tongue. This way you can be relaxed and genuine during networking events, and you'll always be prepared should you meet someone unexpected no matter where you are. You can even use part of your elevator pitch as the intro for your résumé or cover letter, or to kick off an interview should someone ask the dreaded open-ended question, "So tell us about yourself."

INFORMATION INTERVIEWING

Think of an information interview meeting as a networking opportunity. This is a one-on-one meeting with a key person in a field that you have a high interest in.

It may be that you have preconceived ideas about a particular career. Information interviewing can give you a better sense of what it would be like to work in the field you've chosen. It is first-hand, realistic, information you can use to inform your idea of your ideal career.

An informational interview is less formal than a real interview. It allows you the opportunity to show off your personality, your skills, interests, and aptitude in a semi-relaxed atmosphere. Because of this, you will likely come across as more authentic to the interviewer. An informational interview gives a prospective employer better insight into who you are, and how you might be a good fit for the organization in the near future. This is a win-win situation for everyone.

Foot in the door

At the typical interview that follows an application, you might feel that you're in an interview mill—the interviewer bored with all the candidates and simply saying, "Next. Next," after each interview. This may leave you feeling less than confident in your ability to outperform the next person. With an information interview, you aren't going to be competing for a time slot, and chances are the interviewer has 15-20 minutes they can carve out of their busy day to talk shop. Many people enjoy this opportunity to talk about themselves, and about how they got to where they are, as well as to help young job-seekers find a springboard from which to launch *their* careers.

Because informational interviews are less formal—and stressful—the conversations usually flow easier. Remember, you aren't there to ask for a job. You're only there to learn. You want information that will help guide you in the direction of the career best suited for YOU. This means you are the one in control of the questions and the outcome of the interview. This is a great time to let your guard down a little, let your true personality shine, as well as briefly showcase how your skills benefit the company. You can also take the opportunity to ask more strategic questions—questions that help you, but perhaps would not be appropriate at a real interview. You can ask about benefits, salary, and even the social climate of the organization without portraying yourself in a negative light.

Gain Insight, and Practice Interviewing

This is the opportunity for you to come in prepared to ask the right questions. People enjoy telling their story and you can get a real sense of what the company or career might be like, and so determine whether your chosen career is truly a good fit for you.

Additionally, if some parts of the interview process intimidate you, this is an excellent way to come up with a game-plan and practice. Remember practice ONLY makes for improvement.

Mentorship

If you feel a connection with the person you meet with, you may well have lucked into a mentoring relationship opportunity. Your interviewer might really be impressed with the initiative you show by requesting an informational interview, and may be willing to offer further advice and support. And this goes both ways. Because of the rapport you build in this interview, you yourself might ask for further guidance via follow ups which we'll talk about later in this chapter.

How to Conduct Yourself at the Interview

- You should regard each interview as a business appointment and conduct yourself in a professional manner.
- Write a THANK YOU NOTE to the people you have interviewed. Report back to them if you have followed up on any suggestions.

The last thing to remember is that informational interviews are extremely effective. How effective? According to Dr. Randall Hansen, founder of Quintessential Careers, one of the oldest and most comprehensive career development sites on the web, "While one out of every 200 résumés (some studies put the number as high as 1,500 résumés) results in a job offer, one out of every 12 informational interviews results in a job offer."

Informational interviews are so effective that despite that the stated aim is NOT to get a job, almost 10 percent of informational interviews still result in a job offer.

CHAPTER 12
THE RÉSUMÉ

No matter what job you have in life, your success will be determined 5% by your academic credentials, 15% by your professional experiences and 80% by your communication skills.
– Stephen Wang

The goal of a résumé is to communicate who you are, and how you stand out. It is used to express your unique experiences, abilities, skills, as well as your accomplishments. Employers typically spend less than 30 seconds looking at a résumé, so it's very important that your résumé stand out visually and that you utilize, strong, succinct words. Take time to ensure you are conveying exactly what you want the employer to know about you as quickly as possible.

BASIC DOS AND DON'TS OF A GREAT RÉSUMÉ

Let's get started with some simple directions.

Do

- Check for mistakes. Always let your résumé rest for at least fifteen minutes, and then review it again for typos, before sending it off.
- Personalize each résumé to specific positions, even if you are applying to many simultaneously. Often small tweaks—the skills and experiences you emphasize for instance—make a huge difference to whether a potential employer sees you as a good fit.
- List all relevant skills. As mentioned above, which skills are relevant depends on the position you're applying for.
- List the correct contact information and a professional email address.
- Keep your format simple and professional.
- Focus on what you **did** for your previous employee.
- Address and prioritize your most relevant experience for the role you are applying to fill.

Don't

- Copy chunks of texts from the job posting.
- Apply to a company from which you were just relieved.
- Exaggerate hobbies. Do not such describe your recreational pursuits as *professional* experience.

These are some of the most common mistakes reported by employers. If you can avoid them you are a step ahead of many.

Length

One Page:
- Targeted, succinct, and uncomplicated.
- Most for-profit businesses drastically prefer a one-page résumé

with a one-page cover letter. Employers often have many résumés to sort through, and if they are not convinced on the first page they are unlikely to read any subsequent pages. A one-page résumé is viewed as considerate of the employers' time.

More than one page:
- Specific industries may want a more in-depth look at your experience. Government-funded jobs, for example, may want to see more details and the full extent of a candidate's work experience before deciding who to call for interviews. These résumés may be as long as five pages.
  If you are unsure what the most appropriate length is, research the industry standard.
- Provides the employer with extensive details regarding experience and achievements.
- Great for job seekers with many job-relevant skills and experience to share.

Curriculum Vitae (CV)
- In specific industries such as research or art, you are expected to have a list of publications or showings. Instead of cluttering a résumé, attaching a simple CV is much cleaner and professional. This allows potential employers to track down more of your work if they desire.
- If you are uncertain what is expected or whether additional information would be welcome, you can attach a CV or a longer format résumé along with the succinct one-pager. Clearly label the packet with a note that you have sent in both a résumé and a longer format CV should they need additional information.
- Another way you can approach this is to send a one-page résumé with a note that you can send a longer document of your achievements and work history upon request. If you do not hear

back within a week, call or email and gently remind the hiring manager that additional details are available upon request. This shows that you are interested in the job, and gives the recipient another opportunity to remember your name.

Photos

Experts still debate whether a photograph is a good addition to a résumé. Consider the following questions:

- Does this role require me to brand myself?
- Is selling my personality a key component to this job?
- Do I see many people in the same or similar role adding a photo of themselves on business cards, letterheads, and other company stationery?

If the answers steer towards yes, a photo may be worth considering.

If you're adding a photograph, it is always a good idea to hire a professional photographer. While selfies might be fine for social media purposes, a higher standard of professionalism is expected on résumés.

Any photograph should also depict you in career-relevant dress and setting.

THE FORMAT

Depending on your experience and the position you intend to apply for, certain formats may work better for you than others. Each one has strengths and weaknesses. The most important factor is how to highlight how you would most effectively fill the employer's needs.

You'll find examples of each type of résumé at the end of this chapter.

The Chronological Format résumé

Chronological résumés are the most common and easiest to write. You list work experiences in order, from most recent, and describe your responsibilities in previous positions. This type of résumé tells the reviewer what you did in the past but may have little to say about what you can do in the future. If you have had many jobs, it isn't necessary to list them all—list only the most recent and relevant to the job you are applying for.

Advantages:
- Highlights a record of steady employment
- Expected by many employers
- Easiest to prepare
- Highlights companies you have worked for that have a good reputation

Disadvantages:
- Often does not focus on skills
- Emphasizes job hopping
- Emphasizes large gaps in your work history

The Functional Résumé

The functional résumé emphasizes qualifications—skills and accomplishments as opposed to dates, positions, and responsibilities. The content focuses on the objective indicated at the beginning, the applicant's skills, and the prospective employer's needs. It essentially tells prospective employers what you can do for them.

Functional résumés are very useful for individuals who do not have a great deal of work experience, for individuals who have job hopped, and for individuals who have large gaps in their employment history. A chronological résumé would accentuate the fact that you have moved from job to job or have not worked steadily, which may not be to your advantage. Functional résumés are more difficult to prepare because you need a good understanding of both your skills, and the skills that would interests a prospective employer.

Advantages:
- Emphasizes skills and accomplishment
- De-emphasizes spotty job history or frequent job changes
- Focuses on what you can do rather than what you have already done

Disadvantages:
- Is not familiar to employers, who may feel something is missing
- Provides no opportunity to highlight certain employers
- Offers no clear work history

The Combination Résumé

This combines the best characteristics of the chronological and functional résumés. The combination résumé may be more difficult to write. It contains a brief employment history presented chronologically, and stresses skills and competencies, including job titles and dates. This type of résumé allows you to stress your qualifications and work history in chronological and functional terms.

Advantages:

Provides what employers are used to seeing—work history as well as skills and accomplishments

Provides employer with relevant dates in your work history so they can determine how long you stayed at previous jobs, and whether there have been significant gaps in employment.

Disadvantages:

A little more difficult to format into a single page

CHOOSING THE BEST FORMAT

If you have little work history, or frequent jobs over a short period of time, I recommend using the Functional résumé. These days employers tend to be more focused on what candidates can do now. Hiring practices have trended away from an expectation that a candidate will spend 20 years at one organization.

This trend works in concert with another shift—employers finding more and more competitive ways of retaining employees due to the high turnover rates in the majority of the employment marketplace. It costs companies a great deal of money to advertise, hire, and train new employees. So, in general I tend to favor the functional résumé.

WHAT ANY RÉSUMÉ SHOULD INCLUDE:
Your résumé should clearly communicate your major strengths, not just your educational achievements, and your work history. Draw from the skillset strengths you identified in Part I.

It should state your objective—what you want to do for the employer. This is the most important statement on your résumé and it should stand out.

It is often a good idea to include a "Summary of Qualifications" section after stating your objective. A Summary of Qualifications is a list of three to five qualifications. It helps the reader focus on the skills the applicant would bring to the position.

A high impact résumé will be brief and to the point, containing just enough information to persuade the employer to call you for an interview.

For a winning résumé, cite specific examples that illustrate the *results* of your efforts and accomplishments. Wherever appropriate give specific quantities or numbers.

Your résumé may include special awards, and training, particularly if they are relevant to the job for which you are applying.

Your résumé should not contain any reference to salary expectations. Discuss salary at the interview stage—preferably at a second interview unless the potential employer brings it up in the first interview.

Include references to hobbies or interests only if they strengthen your job qualifications. Employers are more likely to be interested in hobbies that involve job skills, community service, or competitive distinctions, as these can speak to employees' skills or their motivation to contribute and perform.

References should be supplied at the time of the interview and should not be listed on your résumé unless requested ahead of time. Your résumé may contain a statement that references will be available on request.

Your résumé should be appealing to the eye and should not be crammed with information. When formatting your résumé leave plenty of white space, use bullet points, and underline headings for emphasis.

It is a good idea to have printed copies of your résumé on hand when attending interviews. Print on high quality, heavy-weight, paper to give your résumé an additional sense of importance, though printing on cardstock is likely going too far.

Consider the company's style, especially if you are in a creative field such as graphic design or marketing. You may consider formatting your résumé or using colors and fonts that mimic those used by the company you're applying to. You might visit the company's website to get an idea of the company's visual brand.

Personal information (age, race, sex, marital status, gender identity, and number of children) is inappropriate on a résumé. In fact, anti-discrimination laws make it inappropriate for employers to ask about these topics in interviews.

Never add clip art.

If you are having trouble finding the words to describe your skills look back at the skills section of the book or consider the following descriptors directly from the U.S. Department of Labor's O*Net Online website

- Active Listening — Giving full attention to what other people are saying, taking time to understand the points being made, asking questions as appropriate, and not interrupting at inappropriate times.

- Reading Comprehension — Understanding written sentences and paragraphs in work related documents.
- Complex Problem Solving — Identifying complex problems and reviewing related information to develop and evaluate options and implement solutions.
- Judgment and Decision Making — Considering the relative costs and benefits of potential actions to choose the most appropriate one.
- Speaking — Talking to others to convey information effectively.
- Oral Comprehension — The ability to listen to and understand information and ideas presented through spoken words and sentences.
- Oral Expression — The ability to communicate information and ideas in speaking so others will understand.
- Written Comprehension — The ability to read and understand information and ideas presented in writing.
- Written Expression — The ability to communicate information and ideas in writing so others will understand.
- Deductive Reasoning — The ability to apply general rules to specific problems to produce answers that make sense.
- Getting Information — acquiring information from all pertinent sources.
- Establishing and Maintaining Relationships — Developing and maintaining productive and collaborative professional relationships
- Making Decisions and Solving Problems — Analyzing information and evaluating results to choose the best solution and solve problems.
- Analyzing Data or Information — Identifying the underlying principles, reasons, or facts of information by breaking down information or data into separate parts.

- Communicating with Persons Outside Organization — Communicating with people outside the organization, representing the organization to customers, the public, government, and other external sources. This information can be exchanged in person, in writing, or by telephone or e-mail.

A strong résumé is vital, to getting an interview. But before someone looks at a résumé they will first be looking at the cover letter. We'll look at cover letters in the next chapter.

Chronological Example

Chef Annie Morris
01234 Apollo Lane
(970) 892-3330
canniem@gmail1.com

Objective: Professional Chef with over 10 years in the food and beverage industry seeking a challenging and fast past environment to showcase gastronomical talents and creative techniques while using local farm products, implementing seasonal ingredients and modern techniques in an environment that promotes a positive work culture.

PROFESSIONAL EXPERIENCE

Executive Palace   Denver, CO
Executive Chef   2014 – Present
Managed daily kitchen operations

- Budgeted daily orders and cut operating costs in first year by 15%
- Repurposed menu to accommodate local farm to table partnerships
- Supervised all food prep and safety protocols
- Manage staff of 10 kitchen workers which included hiring and firing
- Implemented reduced waste concept to staff and dining to promote a "green dining experience"
- Best of Denver Restaurant award for 2016 and 2017

The Room Aspen, CO
Chef 2010 – 2014

- Designed seasonal menus for upscale clientele
- Managed back end of restaurant with 6 employees and scheduling their work week
- Managed and maintained excellent relationship with vendors and suppliers.
- Created a local following with a "Meet the Chef" campaign that gained recognition in local paper

EDUCATION
Chicago Culinary School of Art, Chicago IL
Associates Degree in Culinary Arts June 2009

ADDITIONAL TRAINING
- Internship with The Food Network on up and coming chefs of America Spring 2009
- Under-chef to international chef Anthony Bourdain Summer 2009

References furnished upon request

FUNCTIONAL EXAMPLE

Chef Annie Morris
01234 Apollo Lane
(970) 892-3330
canniem@gmail1.com

Objective: Professional Chef with over 10 years in the food and beverage industry seeking a challenging and fast past environment to showcase gastronomical talents and creative techniques while using local farm products, implementing seasonal ingredients and modern techniques in an environment that promotes a positive work culture.

Summary of Qualifications
- Best of Denver Restaurant award for 2016 and 2017
- Managed daily kitchen operations
- Budgeted daily orders and cut operating costs in first year by 15%
- Re-purposed menu to accommodate local farm to table partnerships
- Supervised all food prep and safety protocols
- Manage staff of 10 kitchen workers which included hiring and firing
- Implemented reduced waste concept to staff and dining to promote a "green dining experience"
- Designed seasonal menus for upscale clientele
- Managed back end of restaurant with 6 employees and scheduling their work week
- Managed and maintained excellent relationship with vendors and suppliers.
- Created a local following with a "Meet the Chef" campaign that gained recognition in local paper

Skill Highlights

- Multitasking in fast paced environments with ability to make quick decisions
- Cleanliness systems to maintain highest quality kitchen
- Attention to detail for high standard presentations of culinary designs
- Business knowledge for the ability to Run software management system for inventory control
- Creative and Competent in Adobe design studio for menu changes

EDUCATION

Chicago Culinary School of Art, Chicago IL
Associates Degree in Culinary Arts June 2009

ADDITIONAL TRAINING

- Internship with The Food Network on up and coming chefs of America Spring 2009
- Under-chef to international chef Anthony Bourdain Summer 2009

References furnished upon request

COMBINATION EXAMPLE

Chef Annie Morris
01234 Apollo Lane (970) 892-3330 canniem@gmail1.com

Objective: Professional Chef with 10+ years in the food and beverage industry seeking a challenging, fast-paced environment to showcase gastronomical talents and creative techniques using local farm products, seasonal ingredients & modern techniques in an environment of positive work culture.

Summary of Qualifications

- Best of Denver Restaurant award for 2016 and 2017
- Managed daily kitchen operations
- Budgeted daily orders and cut operating costs in first year by 15%
- Repurposed menu to accommodate local farm to table partnerships
- Supervised all food prep and safety protocols
- Manage staff of 10 kitchen workers which included hiring and firing
- Implemented reduced waste concept to staff and dining to promote a "green dining experience"
- Designed seasonal menus for upscale clientele
- Managed back end of restaurant with 6 employees and scheduling their work week
- Managed and maintained excellent relationship with vendors and suppliers.
- Created a local following with a "Meet the Chef" campaign that gained recognition in local paper

Skill Highlights

- Multitasking in fast paced environments with ability to make quick decisions
- Cleanliness systems to maintain highest quality kitchen
- Attention to detail for high standard presentations of culinary designs
- Business knowledge for the ability to Run software management system for inventory control
- Creative and Competent in Adobe design studio for menu changes

Work History

2014 – Present   Executive Palace, *Executive Chef* Denver, CO
2010-2014   The Room, *Assistant Chef* Aspen Colorado

EDUCATION

Chicago Culinary School of Art, Chicago IL
Associates Degree in Culinary Arts June 2009

ADDITIONAL TRAINING

- Internship with The Food Network on up and coming chefs of America Spring 2009
- Under-chef to international chef Anthony Bourdain Summer 2009

References furnished upon request

CHAPTER 13
THE COVER LETTER AND OTHER SUBMISSIONS

If you want to be seen, you have to put yourself
out there –it's that simple.
– Karin Fossum

THE COVER LETTER

It is important to include a cover letter with a résumé to show how serious you are about a job. Your cover letter is an opportunity to explain why you're interested in this particular job, and what makes you an exceptional candidate.

Your cover letter shouldn't be too long. One page is most professional. It should not merely re-state your résumé, though you can use it to explain which past job duties specifically prepare you for the job you're applying to.

You can also use your cover letter to (very) briefly explain any personal circumstances that may make a more compelling case for why you're the right person for the job.

If you have a powerful personal experience that makes you particularly passionate about this career field, or personal circumstances that explain a gap in employment (for example, I once had an employee who was unable to work for six months due to injuries sustained in a car accident), this is an opportunity to give your potential employer insight into things that do not have a place on a résumé.

Review the job description and see whether there are a few key requirements you can highlight in the cover letter. With the advent of automation, a company might use software to scan cover letters and résumés for keywords that match what the company is looking for in a candidate. This is especially true for larger companies utilizing large posting pools on the internet.

What you should be sure to do:

- Make sure the person who reads the letter knows why you are writing, what you want, and what your qualifications are.
- Include your phone number, email address, city and state
- Include the date you send your cover letter
- Include some industry terms where appropriate
- Proofread for spelling and grammar
- Type. Do not handwrite.
- Whenever possible, do not use a generic greeting such as, *Dear Sir, Dear Madam; Dear Hiring Manager.* Take the time to find the right person who will be interviewing for the position.
- Avoid using abbreviations and acronyms. You want to come across as a professional.
- Do not include your photograph

Generally, a cover letter follows a simple three-paragraph format:

The first paragraph states why you are writing to the company. It is a good idea to reference how you came to learn about the job. Include the position you are applying for, and state that you have attached a résumé for their review.

The second paragraph should point out at least two qualifications from your résumé that directly pertain to the job posting. When helpful, include additional descriptions such as "in this position I worked with X population" (if the population is the same as the job you are applying for), or "in this position I performed X, Y, and Z duties" (again, where these duties are relevant to the job you're seeking).

I have read complaints from employers who are astonished that the job seeker never referenced how they fit the job description. In fact, some people use their cover letters to say things completely irrelevant to the job they are applying to, or to list inapplicable skills!

Keep to the specific requirements and duties of the job description. Be sure to demonstrate that you know something about their industry, clients, or business.

The third paragraph is where you thank them for their time, and ask them to take next steps.

Do not be afraid to ask them to get in touch with you to set up an interview. It shows enthusiasm and a determination to get the job. This can set you apart from the person who only thanked them for taking the time to look. It is even a good idea to let them know that you will be getting in touch with them as well to see whether they had time to review your résumé. This gives you an opportunity and excuse to contact them and put your name out there one more time.

Be creative, bold, and confident, and you will get noticed! If clients are unsure what to include, I suggest having a generalized cover letter ready to go for the industry where they are seeking employment. Then as, opportunity presents itself, personalize it to the unique skills, mission statement, and clientele of the particular employer where they intend to apply. This can save a lot of stress when you are trying to apply for several jobs at once. Customizing your standard résumé and your cover letter for each position should only take a few minutes.

You'll find an example cover letter at the end of this chapter.

LETTERS OF RECOMMENDATION AND REFERENCES

Most often, I suggest that you include a statement at the end of the résumé that you will provide references and recommendations upon request. This is the standard unless your potential employer specifically requested you submit references with your résumé. If they haven't, know it is common practice for them to ask later in the screening process. It is important to have them ready.

Who should you go to for letters of recommendation?

The obvious answer would be any former employer. While this sounds easy, many people feel out of touch with past employers and seek other ways of developing a resource for letters of recommendations. Many qualified people can speak about your competencies. Think through the people in your life that know your work habits, values, tendencies, and personality traits.

Some examples of people that may be a resource for you are co-workers, business owners, partners, volunteer supervisors, and individuals who have known you for a long time. Good recommendations do not need to say explicitly that you would be the perfect candidate to hire. It is better to take a non-direct approach and ask people to comment on your personal strengths.

Go back to the beginning of this book where I ask you to identify what accomplishments and skills other people see in you. Who were these people? Are they good ones to approach? If you know a specific trait that you would like to highlight, it is perfectly normal to ask someone to speak to those traits and any others they see in you. This can often give someone some guidance on what he or she will write about you.

PORTFOLIOS

If you are in a field that requires someone to see your artistic abilities—graphics, writing, architectural designs, teaching—a portfolio may be a good visual addition to your cover letter and résumé.

People often come to interviews with large folders containing finished pieces that showcase their abilities. If you are in one of these fields, and haven't already, I highly suggest taking the time to create a relevant portfolio. Take high quality photos along with any digital files and create an online portfolio to highlight your work.

Even if you are not particularly tech-savvy, web services such as eMaze, Prezzi, Squarespace, and Wix have streamlined the process to be nearly as easy as a Facebook update. This gives you the ability to send a visually appealing portfolio to your prospective employer ahead of time.

They can review beforehand, and then you can go over it again with them in person. This is sure to leave a lasting impact and give them the opportunity to share it with other people within the organization for input. This is a very professional and contemporary way to demonstrate your ability, and the quality of your work.

While it is not necessary to include a letter of recommendation or portfolio with the initial application, you need to have these prepared. That way, if the prospective employer likes what they have read about you and wants to continue the screening process, you are able to oblige and continue wowing them.

In any case, an archive of letters of recommendation and material for a portfolio should be a continual process. This can be daunting to do last minute and cause unnecessary stress before you even get to the normal stress of preparing for an interview.

Annie Morris
01234 Apollo Lane, Denver, CO
(970) 892-3330
canniem@gmail1.com

September 3, 2018
Mr. John Interviewer
001122 West Work Ave.
Denver, CO 030011

Dear Mr. Interviewer,

I am very interested in your current position opening of Head Chef for your award-winning restaurant. I am an experienced Chef with a history of improving operations at the restaurants where I've worked.

You can see that I have managed and operated key operations factors of fine dining restaurants. A few highlights of my résumé include:

- Award-winning menus
- Innovative promotional techniques
- Reduction of back-end restaurant costs by 15%
- Keen attention to detail within a fast past environment

I'm confident that my creative culinary skills and business sense would be an asset to your company. I have many examples of menu plans I have designed for past employers, and would be happy to share them with your during our interview.

Thank you for your consideration. I look forward to discussing how I could be a fit for you restaurant soon.

Sincerely,
Annie Morris

CHAPTER 14
INTERVIEWING AND NETWORKING BASICS AND BODY LANGUAGE

A good stance and posture reflect a proper state of mind
– Morihei Ueshiba

Would you go somewhere without knowing something about where you were going or what you were going to do there? Wouldn't you want to know what you could expect to happen and possibly how you should present yourself?

Think of a situation where you went someplace and felt underdressed or unprepared to interact with the group of people there because you didn't have any background information about the people, or venue. A job or job interview can be the same way. It's worth a little research on your end so you can have the best possible experience at the potentially new job.

Tips for successful interactions:

- Make sure to research the interviewer/company
- Visualize and rehearse possible interactions
- Practice tough interview questions beforehand
- Research Earnings Calls, Quarterly Reports, & Blog Posts
- Clean up your Facebook & Twitter
- Find something in common with people you know you will meet
- Put thought into your appearance
- Make sure you are well groomed and your clothes are clean
- In a formal interview aim to dress just slightly better than the role you'd have
- Suit jackets are appropriate for all high-level jobs
- Mimic the way the office culture dresses
- Do not wear heavy fragrances
- Make eye contact and listen
- Practice a confident handshake and warm smile
- Pay attention to your posture, stand tall and keep gestures open
- Show genuine interest
- Mirror the interviewer's body language
- Do not flirt. Period. Ever. This is a professional interaction.
- Plan your interview for midweek not Monday or Friday when most people are stressed or distracted
- Arrive early enough to sit, relax, get a sense of the surroundings and recall your preparations
- Take notes
- Don't ask about money, benefits, an office tour, or overtime
- Follow up

Tips for the actual interview:
- Do not dominate the conversation. Respond to questions and wait for the next one. Try to have a dialogue that is somewhat even.
- Don't chew gum or snack. Be professional.

- Come prepared to ask some questions. Make these relevant to duties and responsibilities of the job, as opposed to questions about your benefits, vacations, breaks, etc.
- Don't ask about the salary. It's considered poor business tact. Some employers will ask about your expectations in the first interview, if they know they can only afford a certain salary range. But unless you are asked, it makes sense to interact with them as much as possible, and make them want you as much as possible, before you state your requirements.
- Turn your cell phone off. If you have silenced it instead, DO NOT look at it until AFTER the interview is over.
- Try to understand the timeline before you leave. That is, when will the decisions be made for this position? Some companies may make hiring decisions within a matter of hours or days, while others may have an interviewing and human resources process that takes months. This information will allow you to follow up by phone and ask about the status of the opening. Don't make a pest of yourself, but one follow up phone call is appropriate if the timeline has passed.
- Write a thank you note immediately. It illustrates your attention to detail, as well as your thoughtfulness.

UNDERSTANDING BODY LANGUAGE

Body language defines non-verbal communication. It includes facial expressions, body posture, gestures, eye movement, and use of space. Combinations of eye, eyebrow, lip, nose, and cheek movements help communicate an individual's moods (happy, sad, depressed, angry, etc.).

Body Postures
- A person leaning forward and nodding their head with the discussion implies that they are engaged and very interested in

what is being said.
- Crossed legs and arms, foot kicking slightly implies impatience and emotional detachment.

Gestures

Folded arms are normally not a welcoming gesture. This gesture often indicate a closed mind, unwilling to listen to the speaker's viewpoint.

Crossed arms tend to demonstrate insecurity and a lack of confidence.

Shrugs come in multiple forms. The first could mean the person doesn't understand.

Hunched shoulders point to feeling defensive and raised brows are a submissive gesture.

Exposed palms show nothing is concealed.

Relaxed hands show confidence and self-assurance.

Clenched hands show stress or anger.

Hand wringing shows nervousness and anxiety.

Pointing at a person is often viewed as aggressive and rude. An open hand is more acceptable and formal.

The head nod is generally a sign of agreement and a shorthand for "yes."

Covering the mouth suggests uncertainty or thinking hard about what to say.

Handshake
Bad handshakes:

- finger squeezing,
- bone crushing (shaking the hand too strongly),
- limp fish, (shaking too lightly).

The ideal handshake is firm and friendly. The area between the thumb and index finger meet, and one person does not try to dominate or twist the other.

Breathing
Deep breathing is seen as more relaxed and confident.
Rapid breathing is nervous or anxious.

Tone of Voice
High pitched can be seen as nervousness and lack of confidence
Lower Tone can demonstrate command and confidence
Monotone can come across as indifference or lack of enthusiasm for the job

Choosing Your Own Body Language
Forced body language can come off strange and stilted. This is why practicing in front of a mirror is important. You need to be able to see how it *feels* to look warm, friendly, and confident. Practicing can also assist you to fight anxiety. Anxiety may cause you to appear withdrawn.

It is normal for people to feel nervous in social situations, but this nervousness can be interpreted in many negative ways.

If you find yourself getting tense, or thinking negatively, consider box breathing. Box breathing is done by inhaling through the nose four counts, holding the breath four counts, breathing out four counts. And repeat.

For added benefit when you're box breathing, you can concentrate on your intentions or imagine yourself already in the position you are applying for.

CHAPTER 15
INTERVIEW BETTER THAN MOST

Communication – the human connection – is the key to personal
and career success.

– Paul J. Meyer

Interviews can be an intimidating experience even when you feel qualified. Interviews required you to put your best foot forward, and convince the employer that you would be the perfect person for the job.

When I interview, remembering that the person who is interviewing me was once interviewed for their job as well is incredibly helpful. Your interviewer had the same fears and limiting beliefs that you may have. They aren't magically endowed with authority, or better than you—they are just another interviewee, no matter how it may feel.

In addition to remembering that your interviewers are human beings too, practicing is the best way to ensure you ace an interview. Practice interviews with friends who will be honest with you. This is the best way to learn whether you are presenting yourself well—to learn what you could do better, and to get used to answering interview questions.

TYPES OF INTERVIEW QUESTIONS

Generally, interviewers use four types of questions to conduct interviews. Open Ideas, Negative Bait, Knowledge Check, and Character Strengths. We'll examine each one in turn.

Open Ideas

These are open-ended questions designed to see how you formulate an idea and carry through. The interviewer wants to see if you can formulate a complete thought and develop it. They want to see how you communicate. They will be looking at things like eye contact, body language, and general knowledge of the subject they have asked about.

Usually when people get nervous they end up rambling—using many words without saying anything definitive.

Remember to stick to the point, come to the end of the thought, and stop speaking. If possible, propose a solution to whatever problem or situation the interviewer raised. Try not to diverge off into a tangent.

Taking a few moments of silence in an interview is not a sign of weakness if taken to pull your thoughts together. Take a moment before responding to questions, rather than jumping right in and reacting. Employers know the value of an employee who will make sure they have the best answer before they speak or act!

Open Idea questions to prepare for:

Tell me about yourself. Stress your relevant personality traits and skills for the job. Plan three points to address, so that the interviewer feels they have gotten an in-depth picture of you without a long-winded answer.

What are your strengths and weaknesses? During your interview prep, always plan for and prepare two strengths and one weakness—preferably a weakness that can be spun to look good for the industry you are applying for.

What type of boss do you prefer? You don't get to choose your boss, so instead of describing what you "need," show that you are thinking about the success of the company and the company's projects when you answer this question. Make sure to include why you think this type of boss produces better project results in your explanation, rather than just why the kind of boss you are articulating a preference for is more comfortable for you.

What do you hope to be doing in five years? Ten years? The interviewer is looking to see if you are truly committed to this career path, company, or job. To avoid either looking uninterested or overcommitting, focus on your personal growth goals rather than describing the job title you see yourself holding in the future.

Example: I hope that in five years, I'll have gained experience in X and Y skills/parts of this career field. I hope that I'll be able to take on a higher level of responsibility and really take my work to the next level.

Describe your favorite work situation and why. Again, keep your answer focused on how this work situation leads to great results for the project or company, as opposed to how easy or pleasurable the situation is for you.

What are your job goals? Life/personal goals? For job goals, it might be wise to phrase your goals in terms of a skill you bring to the table, such as providing great service to your clients or employers, or strides you've taken to advance your field. For life/personal goals, it might be wise to avoid mentioning a desire to have more kids than you already have. Employers are not allowed to ask you if you plan to have more kids, because some companies have been known to not hire someone due to a concern that a growing family might take up too much of the candidate's time.

We are going to hire one person of 10 candidates. Why should that

be you? This type of question usually comes at the end of most interviews. It might be worded differently, or it might not even be explicitly stated, but the idea remains the same. This is a good time for a summation that clearly states the match between what you know that position calls for, and your skills, abilities, and temperaments.

Do you have any questions for me? Always go in with some questions written down. If they've been answered, indicate that by saying something like, "I did have some questions, but during the course of this interview you've answered them all. Is it all right if I call you later if more questions occur to me?"

Negative Bait
Some people start to feel very confident in an interview, and may become too casual in their answers. You may feel that you have a real connection with the interviewee and when they ask a rather personal negative question, you take the opportunity to be brutally honest.

While it is good to be honest, it is also important to keep portraying yourself in a positive light. Simply complaining about how awful something was, or how badly another person behaved, for example, can give the impression that you're the kind of person who prefers blaming others for problems over taking an active role in solving them.

Instead of complaining, use questions about difficult situations as an opportunity to talk about how they helped you grow, what you learned to do going forward, or how you would have fixed the situation had you been in charge. This tells your interviewer that you are solution-focused, and that you are always looking to see how you can learn from challenges and address them rather than shifting responsibility to someone else. Remember, a typical interview only lasts around 30 minutes. You want those 30 minutes to be full of reasons why they should hire you. Keep it upbeat, positive, and solution-oriented.

To prepare for this interview question, consider past challenging situations, unpleasant jobs, and even situations where you failed, and practice spinning those in a light that shows how much you learned, and how good you are at solving problems. You should probably find a partner to practice this with.

Negative bait questions to prepare for:
Describe the most challenging work situation you ever had. Choose one with a positive outcome, or one where you learned a tremendous amount that you have successfully applied to future situations.

Describe the worst work situation you ever had. Include in your answer one way that you would have improved the situation if you were in charge, and one thing that you learned from that situation that you've been able to successfully apply in future situations

Describe a work situation that you wish you had handled differently. Try to select an answer from earlier in your career. Include in your answer what you learned from that situation, or what you have learned since, that has allowed you to successfully handle similar situations. If your challenging situation did not have a positive outcome, make sure to mention other similar situations that were successfully resolved because of what you learned.

Why did you leave your last job? Keep it positive. The best answer to this sort of question is "I was looking for more ____" (responsibility/opportunity to learn new skills/etc.).

What frustrates you on a job? How do you communicate these frustrations? Frame your frustrations in terms of how the frustrating thing negatively impacts your performance. Show that you're thinking about the project outcome at all times. This is also a great time to show off your communication skills. An employer who is running a productive team will want to know that employees will notify them if something is impeding the team's performance or productivity.

KNOWLEDGE CHECK

If you have done your homework by following the exercises in this book, you know that you are a good fit for the organization you selected, and your knowledge matches the job description that you are interviewing for. This is a good time to have the accomplishments you identified earlier in this book ready to share.

The accomplishments that were very specific, and can quantify your skill are best suited for this type of questioning. Even if the question is about an abstract subject, you can demonstrate the extent of your knowledge by citing specific achievements. Nothing says, "I know how this industry works," like having a real track record for improving it.

If you are interviewing for a sales position and you earned an accolade for exceeding sales quotas in the past, now is the time to share that information. You can even include the dollar or percentage of achievement during the process.

Knowledge Check questions to prepare for:

What can we expect from you in the first three months? This is not asking for you to commit or project how much you money, or sales you may bring in within your first few months. Rather this Knowledge Check is designed to test whether you have a realistic notion of your own adaptation skills as well as an understanding of what is necessary for quality performance on the job you're applying for.

What drives results in this job? This is about asking about how you will focus and do your best, but it is also a good way for them to check to whether you have an idea of how the job, industry, or similar companies function. It, also, demonstrates that you can look at the job from a macro perspective.

What do you expect your references would say about you? Hopefully, you've already contacted your references and/or have letters of recommendation handy. This is more of an interpersonal knowledge check. If you've not spoken to your references specifically about this job yet, try to remember what they used to say about you when you worked/studied under them.

How would people who have worked with you describe you? Select two or three positive adjectives that are relevant to this job, and think of specific things you have done in previous jobs that explain *why* they say those things. Remember, "positive" adjectives don't always have to be warm and fuzzy. Being described as "no-nonsense," "serious," or "rigorous" could be a good thing too in some industries. This is a further knowledge check used to determine if you understand the demands of the job.

Knowledge checks can come in unexpected forms. They aren't always questions. For instance if you are applying for a job that requires meeting people face to face, the interview may be over lunch. They may be watching for business meal etiquette as that will be an important part of the work you do for them. Understand the role you are applying for and consider the job holistically as opposed to individual tasks.

Character Strengths
Interviewers may want to get a feel for how you may fit in with the culture of the organization. Desirable character traits can vary from industry to industry. In tech, for example, more flexible, creative attitudes may be desired, while in finance, competitiveness, and strategic thinking may be valued.

You may be asked questions about your personality, interests, and hobbies. You will be well prepared with a positive, upbeat, knowledgeable response since you will be able to refer to the personal inventory you took in Chapter 3. You should also be careful to include what you know about the work culture of this particular organization, or industry, as well.

Character strength questions to prepare for:

What are your hobbies? What you choose to do in your spare time tells a lot about you as a person. If possible, the hobbies you identify for your interviewer should demonstrate that you have shown leadership, are involved in making the community a better place, or be one where you use job-relevant skills.

What is the most difficult situation/biggest challenge you've faced? Think about a situation that you solved in a way in keeping with the company culture.

Tell us about a time you've failed. This is an excellent opportunity to show how much you have learned from past experiences, and how you would act differently if you faced the same situation in the future.

Describe a situation that you enjoyed, where you used your strongest skills. This is a time to show the employer how much you enjoy using your job-relevant skills. Illustrate the capabilities you listed on your résumé. Have some concrete examples handy of your most relevant capabilities.

In your last job, what made you the proudest? If possible, this is an ideal moment to cite concrete improvements you made in your past job, such as numbers you've improved. It can also be a good time to relate positive reviews from clients, or past employers, or subordinates.

What do you hope to improve upon as you continue in your career? If possible, talk about something that this job or employer could help you to learn, or get experience with.

Why do you think you'd be good at this job? What can you bring to this job that someone else might not be able to? What makes you special? Remember what we've talked about throughout Part I—

make note of two or three personality traits, two or three skills, and two or three experiences that work together to explain why this job would be a good fit for you.

KEEPING A POSITIVE DEMEANOR

It can be difficult to stay positive during an interview, especially if you have had many interviews that did not previously result in offers or follow-ups. We are often unused to rejection in our personal life, so it can be difficult to adjust to the fact that applying to jobs virtually guarantees we will experience many rejections and few acceptances.

Nonetheless, remember that this is how the game is played. Most positions may interview dozens of applicants and can only hire one. Don't be too concerned if you've had a few interviews and no job offers.

However, if you have interviewed many times and received no favorable responses, here are some things that could be creating roadblocks for you.

I would not expect that anyone would find themselves in this position, had that person diligently completed the exercises in previous chapters.

Is this job a good fit for you?

The interview is a learning experience for both the interviewer and interviewee. Listen to what they say about the job, organization, and expectations. Have the jobs you have interviewed for truly been good fits for your goals? Have you left an interview after getting the impression that a company's culture, goals, policies, or personality might not be what you had expected?

If you are finding many interviews hold unpleasant surprises for you, perhaps you ought to investigate whether a *similar job* or type of employer is a better fit for you?

*Are you remaining positive throughout
the whole interview?*

Are you emphasizing your problem-solving abilities and what you learned from experience? Are you complaining about previous jobs, employers, or clients (this is a big no no!)?

This is the time to convey that you are a potential positive attribute to the company. Remember, research shows that employers value emotional intelligence more highly than IQ.

*Are you answering difficult questions
with both honesty and positivity?*

An example might be, 'What didn't you like about your last job?' Rather than focusing on the negative (what you didn't like), focus on the positive aspects of the decision (what you wanted more of; why you felt the need to seek out a new position). As many people in the workforce recognize the trend of shorter job histories, it's less likely they will be alarmed by a résumé that features multiple jobs. Focus on things you gained from your previous employment that will benefit the new job.

How are you presenting yourself and body language?

This an area that many people overlook. This is an incredibly important area. Practice is not just recommended, it's necessary.

Being able to read the interviewer's body language and respond with appropriate clues is very helpful. This is one place you will absolutely need another person to practice with.

PRACTICING INTERVIEW QUESTIONS

I highly recommend that people preparing to interview in a new industry for the first time practice being interviewed by a friend who can give honest feedback about one's answers, and body language. You want to you get used to talking about yourself in a way that makes you desirable to employers.

If possible, you may even wish to see if any friends, or friends of friends, work in the job or industry you are interviewing for. These people can help you know what to expect from an interviewer in the industry, and what sorts of answers employers in the industry might prefer.

You may also wish to consider taping your practice interview, so that you can hear firsthand how you sound while being interviewed. It can be hard to make adjustments to your interviewing tone or confidence *while* you are talking, but replaying a recorded interview afterwards can allow you to study how others hear and see you.

There is so much commonly available information on how interviews are conducted that there is very little excuse to fail to prepare for common interview questions. Interview practice can relieve stress allowing you to be more relaxed and confident. This is especially true if the stakes are high—situations where there is a real urgency to getting employed.

CHAPTER 16
SENSITIVE QUESTIONS AND AWKWARD INTERVIEWS

If people are informed they will do the right thing. It's when they
are not informed that they become hostages to prejudice.
– Charlayne Hunter-Gault

In a perfect world, we would all like to be judged by our aptitude and potential rather than people's preconceptions about us. But sometimes an interviewer or potential employers' preconceived ideas get in the way of seeing the best you have to offer. Gender, race, perceived disability, and other factors sometimes provide opportunities for preconceptions to take center stage.

Stereotypes of people seem endless, and these can be especially challenging when you're trying to get a job. The best we can do is prepare for the sensitive and awkward moments and rise above them.

OBVIOUS DISCRIMINATION

Sometimes we know even before we meet a person there is a good chance they will judge our ability before we've even said a word. This can be due to disability, race, gender, or sexual orientation.

Fortunately, laws and federal regulations make it illegal for employers to discriminate against the disabled, or to ask questions about one's family, religion, and other sensitive areas.

I HAVE A DISABILITY. ARE THERE LAWS THAT PROTECT ME FROM DISCRIMINATION?

Yes. The Rehabilitation Act (RA) of 1973 makes it illegal to discriminate against individuals with disabilities with respect to jobs, public education, and federal benefits. The Americans with Disabilities Act (ADA) makes it illegal to discriminate against individuals with disabilities with respect to employment in the private arena, with respect to state and local governmental jobs, or with respect to qualifications for state and local benefits.

Nearly all large companies/organizations are aware of these laws. However, smaller establishments may not be. These laws are designed to prohibit discrimination against someone who is otherwise an appropriate candidate for the position, education, or benefit. However, they are not intended to guarantee employment for someone who is clearly incapable of handling the assigned work, even after reasonable accommodation.

WHAT IS A REASONABLE ACCOMMODATION?

Example: I am deaf in one ear. Can I still obtain a position as a doctor's receptionist? Is it reasonable to ask for a device for the telephone that enhances the sound for me?

Yes, this would be considered a reasonable accommodation. Reasonable accommodations are those that:

1. Are required to ensure equal opportunity in the job application

process;

2. Enable the individual with a disability to perform the essential features of a job; and

3. Enable individuals with disabilities to enjoy the same benefits and privileges as those available to individuals without disabilities.

The word "reasonable" takes on a relative tone, depending on the size and capacity of the workplace in question. If an individual is deaf in one ear but is the most qualified person to do the tasks at a job, a reasonable accommodation would be for the employer to purchase a telephone device that enhances sound, provided the employer can afford to do it.

This would enable the individual to carry out the tasks in an optimal way. However, if an individual with ADHD requires a private office in order to concentrate and none is available, a private office would not be a reasonable request.

ILLEGAL QUESTIONS ABOUT NATIONAL ORIGIN, RELIGION, FAMILY, AND MORE

It is illegal for an interviewer or potential employer to explicitly ask some questions. These questions are usually connected to discrimination, i.e. they do not determine your ability to perform a job, and employers may develop unfair assumptions based on their answers.

For example, it is illegal for interviewers to ask you about:

- Your age
- Your race or ethnicity
- Your gender, sex, or gender identity
- Your country of origin or birthplace
- Your religion
- Whether you have a disability
- Whether you are married (or other relationship/family status

questions)

- Whether you are pregnant, have children, or plan to have children

It is illegal for interviewers to deny someone a job based on the answers to those questions.

Here are some concerns my own clients who went job interviewing brought back to me:

I went on a job interview and was asked how old I was, how many children I have, and what my estimated monthly income is. Do I have to give out that kind of information?

No. All of the above are illegal questions. An employer no longer has the right to ask personal questions that don't apply to the work being discussed. The law states that it is illegal for an interviewer to ask you questions related to sex, age, race, religion, national origin, or marital status, or to delve into your personal life for information that is not job related.

IF I AM ASKED AN ILLEGAL QUESTION, HOW SHOULD I ANSWER IT?

You might feel like saying something like, "That's an illegal question, and I don't have to answer it." However, in the real world that probably wouldn't leave the employer with a positive feeling about you.

Instead, decide to what extent the question bothers you. If you don't want to answer at all, you are well within your legal rights. However, if you still want to be considered for the job despite the fact that question was asked, you may want to consider a softer approach.

A good alternative is to try to determine *why* the question is being asked. Is the interviewer concerned that having a family or a disability might make you less available for the job? Are they concerned that you might not be fluent in English if you are from another country? Craft an answer that addresses the underlying concern, rather than simply avoiding the question.

For example:

Interviewer: "Do you have young children?"

Job-seeker: "You are probably wondering whether I have any responsibilities at home that would interfere with my ability to be reliable on the job. I can assure you that I don't. In fact, I received an award for perfect attendance at my last job."

Job-seeker: "I have two little ones. My spouse/parent/daycare takes such great care of them."

Or

Interviewer: "What would you estimate is your household monthly income?"

Job Seeker: "I understand that this job pays with commission only. If your concern is whether or not a cash flow method would work for me, I would prefer base salary plus commission or base salary plus bonus incentive. However, I prepared a financial plan and I've determined that I can handle the cash flow method of commission-only pay as a well."

What About Health Issues?
Do I Have To Tell My Employer About Them?

Generally, no. There are a few exceptions where job duties may pose a health risk if the employer does not know about your medical history. But most employers are not allowed to discriminate against people who take medication or have health conditions. If you cannot think of a safety reason why your employer might need to know, the question is probably illegal.

In the case of the Armed Services, however, knowing an applicants' health history may be important to ensuring the applicants' health is not endangered on the job. A good review of these regulations can be obtained from the ADDA website at www.ada.gov. The Selective Service system, www.sss.gov, is also a good resource. Occasionally, waivers may be obtained under individual circumstances and might be discussed with an appropriate labor attorney.

Health example question:

Interviewer: "How is your health?"

The wording of this question wouldn't be considered legal. But the questions is vague enough for you to answer without going into detail. You may simply choose to answer:

"My health is good."

There is no dictionary definition of 'good' health, and it is illegal to discriminate against people due to illness.

A more appropriately worded question might be:

Interviewer: "Do you have any disabilities or health issues that would interfere with your performance on this job?"

If the question is worked this way, the answer should always be "no." If you have a condition that really does make you incapable of performing this job, I would hope you determined that before the interview stage!

If you need reasonable accommodation to do the job, then you might consider answering like this:

"No. I have done work like this before very effectively. I will say that I know myself, and I work best when I can take a short walk/break every now and then to refresh myself. I have found that doing that really supercharges my productivity throughout the day."

By anticipating the real question, you might be able to sidestep the illegal question and still speak to the concern.

Again, if you do not want to answer the question, it is within your legal right not to answer. You probably won't get the job though—an outcome you must consider.

It may also be wise to consider that if the employer is asking questions that offend or concern you in the interview, the company may not be the best place you could find a job after all. The interview stage is when the company is trying to woo great employees as much as you are trying to woo them, so consider how the employer treats you in the interview when considering whether you want to work for them full-time.

Remember, too, that while large corporations have human resource departments with professionals who are constantly upgrading their knowledge of employment laws, small companies may be totally unaware of the current laws. Therefore, it may be that they are asking out of ignorance of the law without realizing that certain questions are considered discriminatory.

OFF-COLOR, OR SENSITIVE, QUESTIONS AND PRESUMPTIONS

More often than not, a savvy interviewer will not openly say anything discriminatory. They'll form the question in a way that perhaps could be asked of anyone. They may also try to determine the answers to these questions using "leading questions"—questions that do not actually ask about the illegal topic, but hint at it. For instance asking a woman about her age and young children is likely to be seen as discriminatory. But many people don't even realize the racist connotation of asking a person of color "where are you *really/originally* from?" making it difficult to parse whether the person has a prejudiced agenda or is ignorant.

These are examples of situations interviewees have encountered:

If a person has an obviously Jewish or Middle Eastern last name and the interviewer asks, "How often do you take holiday leave?" that question can be an attempt to determine if the employee takes holidays for a religious observance.

If the employer offers vacation time or holiday time as a policy, you can redirect the question by asking, "You offer X weeks, right?" If an employer officially offers a certain amount of vacation time, they should do so with the expectation that employees will use those days off. Employers that say they offer two weeks' vacation but expect their employees not to use those vacation days may be employers to avoid for many reasons!

Discrimination may not always come in the form of a question. There may be small comments that hint that the interviewer is making judgements about your aptitude in a manner not reflected by your résumé or what you've said.

Interviewer (to an interviewee of East Asian descent): This job requires a lot of written and verbal communication. Would you be more comfortable with a more numbers-oriented task?

Always feel free to answer those questions honestly, to ensure you are placed according to your skills, not according to stereotypes.

WHEN SHOULD I DISCLOSE INFORMATION ABOUT MY DISABILITY?

If it is an obvious disability, it is savvy to discuss it openly, and reassure the prospective employer. If you require reasonable accommodations to perform the essential functions of the job, it is also best to deal with this early. Additionally, if, in the future, you would like to be considered for promotions where you might require accommodations, it may be necessary to disclose your disability.

When discussing an obvious disability or disclosing a hidden one, it is useful to voice and address the concerns your employer might feel.

For example:

"I know that might sound pretty intimidating to you. But for me, it's normal. You've seen my résumé/portfolio, so you know what I can do. I get the job done best when I have <reasonable accommodation>. Would that be something you'd be able to provide in order to hire me?"

If your disability is not obvious and you don't suspect that you will require any accommodations from the employer, then it may not be necessary to discuss your disability at all. If you've identified potentially problematic areas and can modify your method of functioning without the employer's help, then you may not want to disclose the disability at all. In these scenarios you state your needs without a declaration of disability.

For example, if you have attention-deficit hyperactivity disorder and you have problems remembering details, you might use certain strategies that you have found helpful. For instance if employees are required to take turns note taking, but you do not want to say you have ADHD which makes the task difficult you may consider saying, "In meetings I find I get so engrossed I often miss writing down important details. I see that meeting notes are important for the team, would it be alright for me to record the meeting on my phone so I can transcribe it after the meeting?"

Remember, there is no shame in having or disclosing a disability. However, since an employer does not need to know all of the chemical, neurological, psychological, or biological systems of your body, unless your disability impacts your work, why would you want to disclose to a perfect stranger more than they need or want to know? You wouldn't think of declaring that you have diabetes or high blood pressure unless somehow this information was relevant to your job. Just as with diabetes or hypertension, there is no need to disclose disabilities or health conditions that are not relevant to your ability to do your job.

RESOURCES TO FIGHT AND COPE WITH DISCRIMINATION

If you find yourself in a difficult situation with an employer, or feeling anxious about interviewing due to fear of discrimination, you might want to use the internet to search for laws and organizations that apply to your particular situation. Available resources and protections include:

Your own documentation

If you have any concerns about discrimination, harassment, or potential wrongful termination, it is a good idea to document all conversations with your supervisor in writing.

For conversations that happen in-person or on the phone, it is a good idea to send e-mails to the person you spoke to, recapping the conversation, and asking to confirm that you understood correctly. Far from being confrontational, this can be done in a friendly, helpful way with an attitude of wanting to make absolutely sure you are doing your job correctly. By creating an electronic record of all conversations, you ensure that you have timestamped evidence of any inappropriate behavior, and of your own performance, behavior, and understandings.

This communication practice can be a powerful deterrent against problematic actions for employers, who know that anything they say or do to you will be documented in writing, and may be used as evidence against them in investigations or in court if they run afoul of any of the discrimination or worker health and safety laws discussed below.

These "confirmatory e-mails"—emails that document all your conversations with other staff and ask them to confirm that you recorded everything correctly—are also powerful tools *within* a company, such that there is never a case of disagreement over the instructions you were given.

The Equal Opportunity Employment Commission (EEOC)

This organization conducts investigations, and can assist in lawsuits, related to workplace discrimination. This organization offers resources and assistance for discrimination based on race, family or parental status, national origin, religion, sex, age, disability, sexual orientation, gender identity, genetic information, and instances of suspected retaliation against employees who report or oppose discriminatory practices. You can read some of their articles and learn more at https://www.eeoc.gov/.

The Occupational Safety and Health and Administration (OSHA)

OSHA is charged with ensuring that employers do not ask their workers to endure unsafe conditions. They produce resources about the health and safety laws employers are required to adhere to, and provide resources for workers to report violations of these laws. Much of these resources can be found at https://www.osha.gov/.

The Americans with Disabilities Act of 1990 (ADA)
The ADA makes it unlawful to discriminate against a qualified individual with a disability, on the basis of that disability. A disability is defined as a physical or mental impairment that limits a major life activity. More information about the resources offered under the ADA can be found at https://www.ada.gov/.

When faced with an employer's discrimination, or other unfortunate behavior, you get to decide whether to file a complaint with one of these agencies. There are pros and cons to every such decision.

The process of filing complaints and seeing any subsequent investigations or lawsuits through to the end can be time-consuming and stressful, and can sometimes damage a person's prospects for employment or promotion with that particular employer. It is often worth collaborating with a coach or mentor and investigating strategies for improving your situation through your own behavior.

However, taking these measures can be a powerful remedy in cases where your health or earning potential has been seriously compromised, and you want to seek compensation or assure that the same thing does not happen to future employees.

CHAPTER 17
YOUR NEW JOB GUIDELINES AND STAGES

Give yourself permission to feel awkward and uncomfortable in a
new job position, even if you have experience in the same field.
You can however, preparer yourself and minimize the discomfort.
— Wilma Fellman

It is hard being the "newbie" on the job. Getting to know the nuances of the people and management flow of a new work team can be intimidating. Some of the most effective pieces of advice I know for those starting a new job include:

KEEP A LOW PROFILE
Try not to come on too strong in the first few days of new employment. It is best to "take in" more than you "give out." After all, how would it feel to have run an organization for a long time and after you invite a new member in they suddenly have a lot to say about things you established by testing and trying methods this person wasn't even there for?

Assess the social climate at your new workplace. Do people seem to chat with each other? Or do they work quietly until official break time? Don't be critical about procedures or routines. Keeping opinions to yourself initially, allows you to stay wise in your assessment of how things are run and be a respected part of "the team." Stay conservative in your dress and respect the other people's boundaries until you have a chance to establish yourself as a valued employee.

In keeping with this idea, it is best not to ask for any special benefits or time off in the first couple of weeks of new employment. Starting a job on Monday and asking for time off on Thursday for an appointment, may not be the best way to make a good initial impression.

Arrive promptly and leave on or after quitting time. If you must miss time at work due to an emergency, most new employers will understand, depending on the circumstances. However, repeated emergencies could reflect poorly on future performance evaluations.

If you know in advance that you will need time off soon after your start date, discuss this with your employer when discussing your start date. Employers are more likely to understand an appointment that was made before you knew your start date, as opposed to an appointment you made *after* your start date that interferes with work.

EXERCISE YOUR INTERPERSONAL SKILLS

Sometimes, when you are focusing hard on doing a good job, you forget to be social.

Remember that your employers didn't just hire a worker, they also hired a co-worker. It's common sense and good practice to use social greetings such as, "Good morning," and show interest in getting to know your fellow employees if you are given breaks at the same time. If you are introverted or shy, that's fine. You don't have to be a social butterfly. Just a few friendly words spoken to coworkers can help establish that you see them and care about their well-being, rather than that you're being aloof or ignoring them.

In general, try to maintain a pleasant demeanor throughout the workday. Be the kind of coworker that you would want to work with!

BE CAREFUL ABOUT MISTAKES

It's important to try and avoid mistakes. Initially, it might be wise to check your work more often than you normally do. Once you've established yourself as a reliable worker, occasional mistakes will be more easily tolerated.

If you are unsure that the work is correct, but afraid you are being a burden by constantly asking questions, consider if you've used and exhausted all non-personnel resources—employee manuals, written protocols, or even internet search engines—before asking your boss or co-worker for more assistance. Can you refer to your employment handbook? Can you double check the information online or in a company manual? This kind of proactivity reinforces the idea that you are a capable problem-solver.

IT TAKES TIME

Most experts agree that it takes six months to feel comfortable in any new position.

At first, you may be high on the excitement of the new job. After the first few weeks, there may be a dip in your energy because you've been trying so hard and learning so much. Few people can keep that pace forever!

If it takes six months to feel comfortable in most new positions, that is about the length of time it takes for you to be at peak efficiency. It takes a full year for most workers to be at a point where they are performing more than they are learning.

GET THE SUPPORT YOU NEED

When you begin a new job, you should already have some idea of the degree of support needed for optimal job performance or any special requirements you may have. Whether you choose to disclose this initially or not, you can incorporate support into your daily procedure.

If you need to have an adaptive device on your telephone to hear better, you should obtain it. If you need a coach to help you stay focused and organized, reach out to a coach via phone, Skype, FaceTime, etc. If you would benefit from a back support on your chair, you should research where to find one and the cost. Your employer may consider this reasonable accommodation.

You should request any reasonable accommodation you might need from your employer as soon as a job offer is made, so that your employer can begin securing those accommodations before you start work. Requests for disability accommodations *after* you've begun working may be met with resistance.

If you prefer to work behind the scenes to secure your own adaptations yourself, disclosure is not always necessary. Whatever the support you should have knowledge of it, along with specific data, upon starting the job.

Whether to disclose a disability or challenge is a sensitive issue. Give it a lot of thought before you decide to come forth with the information, if at all. You are not obligated to disclose a disability unless you are asking for reasonable accommodations. It is a reality that you run the risk of being cast as less than you are capable of, which could limit your potential and future with the employer.

Find an advisor to guide you through the process. Irrespective of the outcome, you should remain positive. Reassure the employer that you are the right fit for the job and highlight all of the attributes that make it possible for you to perform your duties.

CHAPTER 18
STAGES OF ADJUSTMENT TO YOUR NEW JOB

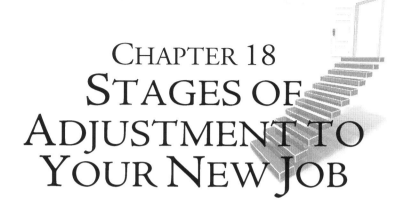

When it is obvious that the goals cannot be reached, don't adjust the goals, adjust the action steps.
– Confucius

Getting a new job can be both exciting and frightening—sometimes each in turn. Often, a job seems exciting and wonderful in the initial stages. Other times, a new employee learns that the new job isn't what they thought it was.

At each juncture, the employee must decide whether their long-term goals will be best-served by staying with the job they've gotten, or whether their new job just doesn't serve their long-term goals.

Here are the stages you can expect after landing a new job:

1. THE HONEYMOON STAGE
Pursuing a new job takes tremendous energy. In most cases, you'll be exhilarated by the hunt, chase, and catch. You won't be able to wait to start the job, and you will dream of how wonderful it's going to be. In

your excitement, you may be slow to recognize signs that perhaps the job isn't the ideal fit for you.

If you have been applying to many jobs, it is likely that you may receive invitations to interview for other jobs, even after accepting one. For this reason, it's a good idea to keep an eye out for things that might prove problematic about your new job, and consider discreetly accepting invitations to interview at other jobs if you see problems with your current job.

You may wish to ask yourself questions like:

- Do employees at this organization always seem stressed out? Do they feel comfortable taking sick days, or do they feel they may be punished for doing so?
- Does it seem like my boss or supervisor is supportive and getting good results, or do they seem disorganized or hostile toward employees?
- Are these job duties going to help me develop the skills and résumé experience for the next step in my career, or are these duties that I don't enjoy or are unhelpful to me?

No job is perfect—most jobs have one or two unpleasant things that you tolerate for the sake of all the other good things. But a workplace where you find that your fellow employees are always stressed out of their minds, where your supervisor is hostile, or where the job duties make you very unhappy, may warrant a look at other jobs and an eye out for better offers.

2. THE "WHAT HAVE I DONE?" STAGE

Eventually all new jobs start to seem a little less exciting as they become routine. Now that we are used to the benefits of the job, the things we find frustrating about it may bother us more. This is normal.

If you find yourself unpleasantly surprised by red flags—unhappiness, major changes to your job duties, or the realization that your supervisor's goals are not compatible with your own—ask yourself the following questions:

- *Am I glad that I'm in this job?* Is it providing me with useful experiences, opportunities to grow my skills, and a reasonable work-life balance?
- *If I am having doubts about whether this is the best job for me, is there a mentor in the field I can talk to about this?* This should be a mentor who does not work for your employer, as companies may immediately start planning to replace an employee if they find out they're considering leaving.
- *Do I want to go back on the job market right now?* For some people, spending a year gaining a reliable paycheck, experience, and a good reference for their résumé can be less stressful than immediately jumping back into job hunting.
- *If I stay here longer, am I likely to get stuck here?* Some organizations can make it difficult for employees to change employers in the future, such as by making the employee feel indebted to the company, or making it difficult to build new skills.
- *How concerned will future employers be if I leave right now?* Leaving within a few months of starting a new job and finding out it's not what you hoped for is usually acceptable. But employers may be alarmed if they see that a worker has changed jobs more than twice in a year, as they may be concerned that such an employee would be likely to leave their company soon after being trained. If you held your last position for less than a year, give serious consideration to potential effects of another quick departure.

3. THE "WHO CAN I BE CLOSE TO?" STAGE

Once you are in a job for the long haul and the novelty has worn off, it's important not to forget about the bonus rewards: all the people you get to work with!

One of the secrets to enjoying a career is enjoying the many friendships that come along with it. It will take some time to get to know others and to establish friendships that are professional and comfortable. Be patient and try not to force this—but be open to ideas like grabbing lunch with coworkers, or going out for drinks on the weekend.

You will be spending a lot of time with these people. You might enjoy it a lot more if you see them as friends. They may also be useful contacts for you in the future, as most of you are likely to go on to different roles and jobs within your career field.

4. THE BALANCING STAGE

Once you have been in your job for more than six months, you will want to ensure that you are also able to enjoy life and pursue long-term goals.

You must continue to learn, work, and play. You must continue to challenge yourself at all three points of balance. If you continuously check the long-term-goals point of balance, you can be sure to offset burnout, lack of challenge, and boredom. This might be a good time to start a new home project, join a new group, take up a new hobby, try out for a community play, or pursue any number of other items on your, "someday I'd love to" list.

Remember that life is a process, not a product. It's not about making your way toward an end goal, it's about making the most of life as it comes. This can include both living with purpose, and accumulating joyful experiences.

WORKING AROUND SPECIFIC CHALLENGES

Internal Challenges

As you start a new job, you may find that you have trouble concentrating, or you feel like you're struggling to learn and keep up. You may also be aware that you have a disability or condition that requires certain provisions for you to focus and get work done.

If you find yourself in one of these situations, here are some suggestions to help you settle into your new work environment:

- Ask to meet with your supervisor regularly for feedback. This will show your supervisor that you are interested in ensuring you are performing well and meeting expectations, and may result in a better alignment of your job duties.
- Ask your employer to reduce distractions in your work environment. It is not uncommon for employers to ask how you best work. That is a good time to bring this up.
- Ask colleagues how they stay organized, and how they streamline their processes. Other employees at the same organization have likely developed tips and tricks to make things run smoothly.
- Ask to use headphones to reduce distraction. This is a fairly common accommodation for motivation and distractions.
- Use to-do lists and checklists to prioritize and keep track of tasks and deadlines. Making and using detailed checklists has been shown to drastically reduce error rates across industries.
- Use post-it notes. Having brightly-colored visual reminders in your workspace can help you keep track when juggling many tasks.
- Set your phone alarm or reminders to regularly draw your attention to things you want to accomplish or prioritize.
- Don't be afraid to seek private office space when you really need to concentrate on a task if you work in a highly distracting area. Most offices have some private area where employees can go if they need to focus on an urgent task.
- Take detailed notes in meetings, or ask a colleague if you can copy theirs. If your jobs involve phone calls where a large volume of information is exchanged, free services on the internet

allow you to record these calls as a sound file. Search the internet for these programs to learn more.

External Challenges

Unfortunately, some people face external challenges in the workplace. These can arise from factors including difficult bosses and discrimination.

If you find yourself in a job that is valuable in terms of advancing your career, but where you feel challenged or disliked by those around you, try these tips geared towards making your time there more bearable and improving your outcome:

- Document all conversations you have about work with your supervisor, colleagues, or clients, in writing, just as we discussed in Chapter 16.
- If you have a phone or in-person conversation, with them, immediately recap the contents of the conversation in an e-mail and send it do them. You can frame the e-mail in terms of "making sure I am understanding correctly."

This can discourage bad behavior because the people you communicate with will know that anything they say to you may be recorded in writing in real time. It will also prove what people did or did not tell you, which can protect against false claims that you failed to follow directions you were never given, or that your supervisor did not know about something you told them about.

- If you find yourself frustrated, feeling ignored, or mistreated, write an e-mail about it—but then send that e-mail to your personal e-mail address, or to a friend or mentor, instead of your boss or colleague.
  After getting feedback from your friend or mentor, or after getting home from work to check your personal e-mails, consider

what you can constructively write in a new version of the e-mail that might improve your circumstances, or whether you should complain about this particular incident at all.

Friends, mentors, and simple distance in time from the incident can help us ensure that we sound professional and calm in our communications. Writing and reviewing e-mails in this way can help us to keep a record of problematic behaviors by colleagues or supervisors—but also ensures that we pick and choose our battles, calmly bringing up serious issues while avoiding looking emotional or complaining about minor things.

When bringing up serious concerns, frame your e-mails from the perspective of how addressing the problematic behavior could be good for the company's business. You may wish to show how your ignored idea would improve the company's capabilities, or how changing systemic problems like an environment that feels intimidating to certain kinds of employees could open the business up to a new, dynamic pool of talent and clientele.

- Self-care. When in an environment that confronts you with hostility or frustrations, it can become easy to believe what the people around you tell you about your capabilities or worth. Take time to do things that make you feel good, and keep referring back to the list of accomplishments we developed in Part I to remind yourself of all of your strengths and accomplishments.

Remember, this job is temporary. Your career goals are not!

The job market may sometimes seem scary—but finding a career that works for you is incredibly rewarding. By being proactive in pursuing your dreams and your personal purpose, you can chart the best course for yourself, and change the world for the better along the way.

Happiness + Passion + Purpose.

ABOUT THE AUTHOR

Michelle Raz, M.Ed. is a Board Certified Coach, Certified Career Coach, executive function specialist, blogger, and owner of Raz Coaching. She serves clients of all ages and walks of life, though she makes a specialty of assisting individuals overcome those cognitive challenges standing between them and their dream career.

After dedicating many years to helping clients overcome their challenges and secure careers they love, she expanded her services to include online-business and career consulting services, and webinars. Now, she is sharing her expertise with readers, in hopes of helping every job-seeker find a career he or she loves.

Visit www.razcoaching.com to find the webinar that follows along with this book and sign up for an interactive experience.

Download your FREE PDF workbook that includes all of these tasks at http://www.razcoaching.com/happiness-tasks

Thanks for reading Happiness + Passion + Purpose.
I hope you loved it.

As an independent author, I count on readers like you to spread the word and support future work. If you enjoy this book, please join the ranks of my readers who make it all possible. You can:

-Write a review on Amazon
https://www.amazon.com/dp/1795530170.
-Subscribe to email updates at https://razcoaching.com/newsletter/
  and be the first to know about future works.

CONNECT WITH ME ON:

LinkedIn: https://www.linkedin.com/in/coachmichelleraz/

Facebook: https://www.facebook.com/yourcareercoachexpert/

Twitter: @razcoaching

Instagram: Raz Coaching

Blog: https://razcoaching.com/blog/

Website: www.razcoaching.com

Please connect, I'd love to stay in touch.
Thanks again,
Michelle Raz

Made in the USA
Monee, IL
04 September 2019